Five Boxes

Five Boxes

Mark MacLean

With illustrations by Trevor Dickinson

HUNTER PRESS

First published in 2015 by
Hunter Press
PO Box 671
Hamilton NSW 2303
Email: publisher@hunterpress.com.au
Web: www.hunterpress.com.au

ISBN: 978-0-9924885-3-6 (print book)

Design and cover illustration: Christine Bruderlin
Interior illustrations: Trevor Dickinson
Printed in Australia by Ligare Pty Ltd.

Contents

AN ATTIC FULL OF STUFF

I'm doing a bit in the allotment next to Dad's house. He used to be out in it all the time but he doesn't bother any more. His lungs are knackered from a lifetime of rollies and working in the building industry and anyway, as he likes to remind everyone, there's no point in gardening because these days you can buy stuff cheaper than growing it. I don't like to see the place untended though and so I've got the scythe from the lean-to and I'm cutting back the dead grass and brambles.

It's a ritual I go through whenever I come home. When I say 'home' I mean the place where I grew up and where my Dad still lives, not 'home' the place where I live now and where my own kids were born and grew up. We've come on holiday from the warmth of coastal New South Wales to this damp corner of northern England, to the pebble-dashed bungalow that overlooks an estuary of bleak, gunmetal-coloured water. It's the Australian school holidays, which is the middle of winter in England, and Dad says, 'Why don't you come over in summer, when it's nice?' And we'll have that conversation again about how the Australian school holidays are in December and January, when it's summer there, and he'll go, 'Aye. Yeah. That's right.'

I'm scything away and dragging the brambles into a pile for a fire later on. Dad's leaning on the wall, silently critiquing my technique, then he goes, 'Put that bloody thing away. It'll only grow back.' I keep scything. We've been through this before, a few times. 'You can buy stuff cheaper in the shops. Come and have a brew.'

So the scythe's back in the lean-to and now I'm not wasting my time, I'm using it more productively by being slumped in front of the telly with a cup of Nescafe and a Penguin biscuit watching a repeat of *Bargain Hunt*. The Red Team pay a stupid amount of money for a snuffbox and we both shake our heads.

Dad says, 'There's some bloody rubbish on these days', and I say, 'Yeah', and then he says, out of nowhere, 'They've come up with a scheme.'

I say, 'Who's that, then?'

He says, 'Government', and makes that 'pfft' sound with his lips, the one that made my blood run cold when it was directed at me over some daft thing I'd said or done.

It turns out the government wants to put insulation in the roof for all pensioners, for free, to keep their energy bills down. Dad's not sure about it. He has the natural suspicion of folk from that generation towards anything that's from government and is 'free'. But they'd been round, these young lads from the government, and had a look up in the cock loft and said they'd be back in a fortnight to lay out the rolls of fibreglass pads.

Before they could do anything with the fibreglass rolls, Dad had to organise to get all the stuff down from up there because they're not allowed to touch it, these government lads. It's the stuff that's been shoved out of sight till someone can decide what to do with it: busted stuff; stuff that's been superseded by newer stuff but isn't bad enough to chuck out but no one else actually wants; stuff that used to belong to folk who lived here for a bit but got left behind when they moved on, always intending to come back and pick it up, but never did.

Dad can barely push a trolley round the supermarket these days, let alone climb a ladder into the cock loft, and so my brother-in-law's been up there and pulled it down, all this stuff, and stacked it in the space next to the central heating boiler. It's mostly bloody rubbish, Dad reckons. An old vacuum cleaner. A set-up my brother-in-law made for Mam so that she could get on and off the toilet a bit easier when she was starting to lose her mobility and we hadn't yet worked out how bad she was going to get. A costume that one of the grandkids wore to a fancy dress party that only ever saw the light of day once but involved hours and hours of work to make and so it somehow seemed a shame just to chuck it in the bin.

And my stuff. The stuff that was in the bedroom when I left home one day and didn't come back.

It's not like I had a plan. I was only going away for a bit, which is what I'd been doing for some time. Go somewhere, work for a bit, come back for a bit, then go somewhere else. I certainly didn't mean to end up in Australia for the next thirty years with two kids and a career and my own attic full of stuff in New South Wales.

Mam and Dad aren't particularly sentimental folk, so as soon as they realised I wasn't coming home in the foreseeable future they pounced. Not for me the shrine-like bedroom kept exactly as it was on the day I lugged my pack onto my shoulders and cadged a lift to the station. There were always folk around who needed a room, people like my sister and brother-in-law who camped out at Mam and Dad's place for a while after they started renovating an old pub. And that's how it should be.

But now my stuff was in the back bedroom by the boiler. They'd had the good grace not to chuck it all out thirty years ago but Dad suggested I do something with it now or it would indeed end up in the skip. I started looking at it a bit, started picking through stuff, and within half and hour I'd filled the wheelie bin. Then I went back to the wheelie bin and pulled most of it back out. It seemed a shame to chuck it away after all these years. But it was mostly rubbish, so I put it back in the bin. Then took it out. And so on.

I couldn't think; I couldn't make decisions. Apart from anything else it wasn't what I wanted to be doing on holiday so I got my laptop out and found a place that specialises in shipping stuff to expats in Hong Kong and the Falkland Islands and Australia. They drop off the folded cardboard boxes and the packing tape, you give them a date, then they come back and pick it up and ship it off to wherever.

So they dropped off the boxes and I filled them up with all my stuff: it filled five boxes. I deliberately didn't look at it too hard, other than to check for solvents and explosives. And the holiday continued for a little longer. We saw the first inklings of the change in seasons. And in time we headed back, me and the kids, back to Australia, and as we pulled away from the house and we waved at Dad I had those usual thoughts about 'Is this the last time I'll see him?' and 'Will I have any reason to come back here once he's gone?' And then those thoughts disappeared in a whirl of airport departure boards and connections and seat allocations and peeling back the cardboard lids on meals in tin foil trays served at odd hours.

And then we were back home, the other home.

* * *

The boxes took about three months to get here. They were pretty knocked about when they arrived, the packing tape that the shipping company gave me had been doubled over by the stuff that Customs use after they've had a snoop inside. The delivery man had an electronic tracking device and I signed for the boxes by scratching my name onto an LCD screen. I lugged them into my office, a tin shed at the end of the garden, and left them there. Then, on a Sunday morning, I started unpacking them.

Unseasonal English-style rain fell outside making the air damp and this mixed in with the musty scent of Dad's attic as I opened one box then another. I hadn't thought the process through and so very quickly the desk and the floor and the shelves and every flat surface was covered in books and records and boxes of photos and slides and Marvel comics . . . and . . . *stuff*.

I picked it up, handled it, put it back down. Wondered about it. Why was *that* thing in the box and not some other thing? Why did *this* piece of stuff get packed into the attic thirty years ago and not some other? Where were the things that I expected to be there? Did I lend them to someone and never get them back? Did they get thrown out? Broken? Sold on eBay by my niece?

It was a flattening experience. This was not a time capsule, or at least it wasn't the time capsule I'd expected. I had not deliberately gathered together, thirty years ago, the things that I thought best represented me at that time for future discovery by middle-aged me. It was just stuff: an arbitrary, unedited collection of things that purely by chance happened to be in my room at the moment I left, and had gotten scooped up and thrown into storage.

The stuff sat there for a few days, crowding up my office, taking up space, smelling stale and English. It sulked at me and I sulked back. Eventually I put everything back into the boxes, if only to get some working space.

I have very distinct memories of my late teens and early twenties. It was the time when I left school, started my apprenticeship as an electrician, left home and came back, travelled overseas, went out with girls, started drinking, had a disposable income, rode motorbikes with packs of other young men, cemented my political beliefs, read the kinds of books and listened to the kind of music that I'd never read or listen to again. I have a very clear image of myself at that time and yet there were some things in the boxes that conflicted with that image.

I wondered: Was I really like the person I remember myself to be? Or does the evidence in the boxes tell a different story? And, if it does, what story does it tell me about me?

There was only one way to find out. I had to go through the boxes systematically, one by one, and re-examine the stuff inside. I'd go through them and retell the story of me, box by box.

And so I started, with Box 1.

Box 1

The house I grew up in was the house that Dad built. The front room used to be two rooms—a living room and a bedroom—but, not long after he built it, he knocked the two rooms into one. Mam died a few years ago and so it's just him in there. He has a chair by the fire (it's a gas fire now, not a coal fire anymore) and from where he sits he can look out of the window and see number 248 over the road, the house where he was born and where he in turn grew up.

After his own father died, Dad and his sisters and his seven brothers bought the derelict barn that was over the road from their house, knocked it down, and on that site built a new bungalow for their mother to live in. This was to become our house. It was handy that there were plenty of brothers in the trade: Dad was a bricklayer, our George a plasterer, Bob a spark, Malcolm a plumber and so on. In 1961, the year I was born, Grandma and Dad and various of the siblings and siblings' friends moved in to the pebble-dashed bungalow that will in my mind always be home. Grandma died that same year and so she never got to experience the house as a home, which in some ways was a blessing.

As I say, Dad was a bricklayer, not an architect. On the MacLean side of the family people are either Vikings (tall, lanky and blonde) or Picts (short, squat and dark). When we pose for family photographs we look like a row of broken teeth. Dad's mother was a Pict—about four foot nothing tall and four foot nothing round—but Dad was a Viking and so the house was built for Vikings. Cupboards were built conveniently, Vikingly, high. It's as though he'd deliberately set out to drive his mother mad. There was a cupboard which, now that I'm older and know about these things, is called a linen press but which I always knew as 'the airing cupboard' because it was next to and above the open coal fireplace. This airing cupboard was where the copper boiler had been boxed in with shelves so that sheets and towels could dry out, but, had she lived, his poor mother would have spent her entire life asking someone to put things up there or get them down for her.

When the fire was well stoked on a winter's night the water would boil and gurgle and lunge about inside the copper so that it sounded like we had the La Brea tar pits in the front room. It's a sound I always link with Sunday nights: beans on toast for tea, a bath, *Tich and Quackers* on the telly or *Sing Something Simple* on the radio, school in the morning. The cupboard below the boiler was the best cubby in the world; warm and dark and you could hide in there, wrapped in old blankets, and spy on the grown-ups through a crack in the door as they smoked cigarettes and watched telly. Once a year Dad would get a new pair of hobnailed boots and the old pair would go on the fire, even though Mam would beg him not to. The blaze those boots could give was fierce and would get the water in the copper roiling and galumphing around, and would usually set the soot in the chimney on fire. It was great fun on a winter's night to run outside and watch orange flames shoot out of the chimney pot. But as Dad said, it was cheaper than getting a sweep in, and if something went wrong he could always build us a new one.

As part of its (non)design the house was cut in two by a hallway that ran the length of the house from east to west and took up more space than any of the actual rooms. It was good for rainy-day ball sports or setting up toy soldiers to be knocked down by golf-ball hand grenades, but that's about it. Uncle Bob wired the place and, because there were so many ill-thought-through points of entry and exit, the hallway had to have a cunning system of light switches positioned every few feet so that you were never in the dark, no matter where you were coming from or going to.

When I think of that hallway I'm taken back to my first memory, of standing at the western end on a Friday night, maybe in winter because the hall lights are on and our Mam, Norma, is at the eastern end, in the bathroom, with the door open. She's got a skirt on that's quite short but it isn't a mini skirt because it's got a top bit that goes over her body (a shift?) and she's looking in the mirror and putting hairspray onto her beehive. She's not just *putting* it on, she's *hosing* it on. Gallons of the stuff, so much so that I can't see the top of her head; where it should be there's a kind of low-hanging cloud of gas-propelled glue. If Dad came in with a rollie the whole house would have gone up in a huge hairspray-fuelled mushroom cloud. There's music and she's singing along so she must be playing singles on the Dansette; it's *Downtown* by Petula Clark, which is a memory that's so precise that it must be untrue.

I'm sure it did happen, or that at least some of it did, though in the memory Mam's wearing the same skirt that she's wearing in a photo of her and me standing outside the house some time in the mid Sixties. We're standing next to the French windows, the ones that Dad pulled out and bricked up because they always leaked when a westerly came off the Irish Sea and pushed rain through the gaps and under the lino. We're both stood upright against the pebble dash—she has her arms hanging loosely at her side and I'm squinting, with one shoulder cocked—and she's got the same beehive, so I'm thinking that there's some kind of crossover thing happening in my memory. And even though I can't see myself, I know that in my memory of standing in the hallway on that Friday night I'm wearing the same brown T-shirt with horizontal white stripes that I'm wearing in that photo.

Inside Box 1 is a smaller box, and inside that box, wrapped in tissue, is a bauble made of the thinnest glass known to man. It's the only one to survive the Christmases of 1965 to 1971. We had a silver Christmas tree made of wire and tinsel, about four feet tall, and each year Dad would get it out of the loft, dust it off and my sister and I would get loops of wool or cotton, thread them through the little clasp at the top of each bauble and hang them from the wire branches. Every year, during the dressing of the tree or pulling everything down, a bauble would shatter. I can't remember being the person who did the shattering, but being a cack-handed little kid it's a fair bet that I was closely involved.

Some time in the early Seventies Dad came home with a real tree, or at least the top six feet of a tree that was now a stump in some Forestry-managed paddock up in the Lakes. We put it in a bucket with a few house bricks to hold it firm then back-filled with building sand. It wasn't a success. It smelt nice and piney but its branches were too irregular; they came out of the trunk at all kinds of odd angles, not like the tinsel tree, which looked like a Christmas tree should look. After a few days the carpet was covered in a fine layer of needles that the push-pull sweeper couldn't pick up. And at night, if we turned the lights off and watched telly in the dark, it didn't have that magic Christmasy sparkle in the light from the coal fire that the tinsel tree had.

We persisted with a real tree for a few more years but we gave up around the time my sister went to teachers' college. Without her drive and energy the whole Christmas thing slipped completely for a couple of seasons. The main decoration became the dozens and dozens of greeting cards that stood up on the mantelpiece or were hung along lengths of wool that drooped around the walls from drawing-pins. They were all for Norma from her mates at the shoe factory. She'd spend ages from late

November writing out cards for everyone and each day in December come home with armfuls of cards that she'd received in return. And Dad would narrow his eyes at them and purse his lips and go 'Pfft'.

When my own kids were little we got a real tree. Christmas in December in Australia can be rather warm and we had the same experience: a nice piney smell followed by hundreds of needles in the carpet. We ended up getting a tinsel tree too, though with a small nod to tradition this one is green. Our baubles are made out of some kind of shatterproof carbon fibre product; you could smack them around the house with a cricket bat and they wouldn't break.

Now this last glass bauble sits in an eggcup on a shelf in my office. I *know* that at some point I'll break it. I just know it.

* * *

Off the long east–west hallway of Dad's house there's another shorter hallway leading to the front door, with the obligatory multiple light switches at regular intervals on the walls. By the front door there are two fat cables where the power comes in to a kind of fuse box that looks like a Cyberman's head.

It's in this hallway where this lampshade hung for years. It's a piece of Fifties tat, the kind of thing that these days you'd see for two dollars in a hardware store. It's made out of pressed metal with clear rippled glass; the shape's that of a pseudo-Chinese lantern. I love it. I'm going to put it up in my office.

Norma loved anything new. Oftentimes I'd come home to find that a perfectly decent and well-loved piece of wooden furniture had been turfed out and replaced by some fibreboard crap from MFI. She loved the future: tinned carrots and tin foil and fabric that generated its own electricity. During the war she was evacuated from a grim, poverty-stricken Catholic home in Salford's docks and—after various hair-raising adventures—was adopted by a couple of strict, childless Methodists.

I don't think you have to have a psychology degree to work out that these things are in some way linked.

I have an old photograph of that lampshade from when it was hanging up in the hall. I must have taken it some time in my teens. I didn't take pictures of all the lampshades (even I'm not that weird), just that one, because I knew that, like everything else in the house, there would come a day when Norma noticed it and that its days would thenceforth be numbered. She'd be off to wherever you bought crappy lampshades in 1981 and get our Dad to pull the lovely old Chinese-style one down and chuck it in the bin.

Somehow it got saved and put up in the loft. And now I have it, and it's in my office.

* * *

At primary school we were divided up into the infants, the juniors and the seniors. Because the school was only about fifty kids there were regular sweeps of the village to sign up anyone who was close enough to school age in order to keep the numbers up and avoid the ever-present threat of closure. So the infants were often just that.

It was when I'd graduated from infants to juniors that I learnt that 'oblong' and 'rectangle' were actually the same thing. I also remember the feeling that somehow oblong was an infants' kind of word and that me, being grown up now, should start saying rectangle. But I've always preferred oblong.

Oblong is the word that best describes the shape of our house and yet our house manages somehow to be higgledy-piggledy, as though it was a smaller house that had bits added on. When they first moved in, there was Mam and Dad in there with my sister and me, as well as his mother and one of his younger brothers and one of his younger sisters, and her German friend who was studying nursing, and so on. It was a tight fit but Dad likes crowds and movement and the constant coming and going of people. There is *always* room for one or two more, there are always cushions being pulled off settees for unannounced cousins to sleep on.

I shared a bed with my older sister, which I don't remember having an opinion about but must have been murderous for her. I remember lying in bed on nights when Mam and Dad had gone out and she was the responsible older sister. When the neighbours' car turned round in their driveway its headlights would sweep across our window and the V-shaped ruffles at the top, where the curtains joined the rings on the pole, would let white light through in jagged rows. We called them the Giant's Teeth and we'd hug together as they swept across the ceiling.

We both wasted lots of hours redesigning that oblong house, the two of us, reconfiguring its endless miles of hallways and strings of cunningly interlinked light switches. I don't know about my sister but the room I wasted the most time in redesigning was not a room at all, it was the huge space above us all that we called the 'cock loft'. I don't even know what a cock loft is; it sounds vaguely nautical.

There are blessed days when you're a kid when everyone else is out of the house and you're the only one at home. You might wander round, go into the normally out of bounds areas like your Mam and Dad's bedroom, stand there looking at their bed and their wardrobe and their stuff, a bit scared in case they come and find you but excited to be in this adult world that feels so utterly different to your own.

My favourite out of bounds place was the cock loft. The hatch was about halfway down the east–west hallway and I'd worked out a way of pushing my back into one wall and walking my feet up the other wall Batman and Robin style, gradually getting up high enough to push the hatch back inside the loft, then doing some crazy monkey bar thing to swing up and into the darkness. If you got the waterproof torch that Dad kept in the airing cupboard (because that made the batteries last longer), the torch he used when he went rabbiting, you could hop across the rafters, looking at the stuff that had been shoved up and out of the way. The cage for Joey, the recently departed budgie, with its tall, red enamel stand and black Bakelite balls for feet. The medieval upright vacuum cleaner with its cloth flex and saggy bag that didn't pick anything up. It was another world up there; it had its own particular silence and yet because of the lack of insulation you could hear cars and lorries going past—the rumble of trucks from the slate quarry and the nee-naa nee-naa of a siren—or the sound of people shouting at each other across the street, the whoops of kids as one of them runs too fast down the hill, arms windmilling and nearly face-plants into the council gravel bin.

Dad's work meant that I sometimes ended up hanging around building sites after school, making islands of the stacks of bricks and jumping from one to another to avoid landing in the shark-infested oceans of the haematite-red slurry between them. Maybe because I'd spent time watching them being built I never really thought of a house as a fixed thing; it all seemed so easily changed. Add a room, take a room off, brick up a window, knock one through. In my fantasy the cock loft had dormer windows, and French doors in the gable end leading onto some kind of balcony affair. Inside, it was one huge room that I could run up and down in. And *it was mine*.

The air in the cock loft is musty and damp, the perfectly wrong conditions for storing anything. Back in my office in Australia I can smell that air in every grain and pore of the comics and the scrapbooks, the photo albums and the record sleeves, when I hold them close to my face and inhale.

* * *

Mam had terrible collections: little wooden display racks with elaborately decorated teapots that were too small and fancy ever to be useful; porcelain figurines of Edwardian ladies twirling parasols; a barrel-organ player with a monkey holding out its cap; glassware like the oversize blue brandy glass with, inside it at the bottom, a forlorn-looking mouse and, hanging over the brim, a very pleased-with-itself cat. I hated the lot of it.

Deep in Box 1 there's a crumbling old plastic shopping bag with little porcelain animals inside. It's not a collection, and I was never much of a collector. To be a collector means having a passion for the thing you're collecting, spending weekends researching its history, searching for and adding good quality and representative samples, swapping and buying and stealing and doing whatever it takes. I tend to just gather things for a while then . . . stop. I've got part of what could have been a good stamp collection, a couple of years' worth of the small A4 posters the Royal Mail produced to promote new editions of stamps, a cardboard box full of beer mats. And these porcelain animals in the plastic bag.

To be honest they look like the kind of thing a teenage girl might collect. I think I got the first one from my sister after she brought it home from a school trip. It's a little hedgehog about two inches long; the bristles are more like ripples in the porcelain but the face is good, a perfect hedgehog face. It sat there for a while on my windowsill until one day I was in a shop and I saw another little figure, this time of a fox. They seemed like such a perfect match, this hedgehog and the fox, and I worried for the hedgehog being all on its own on the cold windowsill that frosted up in the winter. So I bought the fox, which meant that I had two of them and two things means that there must be a third. And when you've got three of something . . .

I went after English woodland animals: an otter, an owl, a squirrel, a trout, a fawn, a duck. But as is so often the case things went wrong. Another person saw the collection, maybe a grandparent who thought, 'Ho ho! Here's a fine opportunity for something small in a Christmas stocking.' I can't remember the exact circumstances but at some point this person or persons got me . . . a lion. Lions do not live in Cumbria. Lions are not considered to be animals of the deciduous woodlands. This lion wasn't even a good lion; it was a bit cacky, poorly moulded with muddy colours. It was made by another company entirely, a bit like how the Hanna-Barbera Tom and Jerry cartoons were perfect but later ones were made by a different studio and in being different they ruined the pleasure of the originals. It was wrong and it spoiled things.

Worse was to come: an elephant appeared, tuskless but with his head thrown back allowing his curled trunk to trumpet joyfully to the heavens. And then a kneeling giraffe.

This was a dilemma, but what to do? In no time at all, or so it seemed, there were as many creatures of the rolling African grasslands as there were the familiar, playful animals of the Lakeland forests. I corralled them into two groups and they occupied opposite ends of the windowsill. It was an uneasy truce that was completely upset by two more arrivals: a second elephant (yes, I know: *two* elephants) and a chimpanzee. The pair of elephants was bad enough because they defied positioning (back-to-back and trunks trumpeting in opposite directions, or facing one another? Side by side or in a line?) but the chimp was impossible. He was terrifyingly out of scale and so if he were real he would have been twice as big as the elephants. He sat cross-legged as though settled in for an hour of Zen meditation but his head was cocked to one side and his eyes squinted as though he were sizing you up. It was like he wasn't really an animal at all; it was like he *knew*.

It was too unsettling for me at the time. I got a plastic bag from the pile we kept in a wicker basket in the kitchen and I put all the animals in there, not to see the light of day for more than three decades.

They seem to have got on all right together. There are no signs of the fox having eaten the hedgehog or the lion and the hippo having had a nasty to-do. But that bloody chimpanzee—as soon as I pulled him out of the bag it was like the last thirty-eight years had never happened.

He's back in there now, for another thirty-eight.

* * *

Like a lot of young men I had little or no idea about how to talk to girls. Well that's not completely true. *At a certain age* I struggled to talk to girls. At school there were girls who were very good friends and my company was mixed. I can see where they've written their names in my schoolbooks and I probably wrote mine in theirs but there was a transition period around school-leaving and the first years of my apprenticeship where my world became almost exclusively male. A few of us lads were a bit of a pack and we all yearned for the company of girls but, in our efforts to achieve this, we somehow gathered ourselves into an even closer-knit group that was never going to attract females. In fact they probably saw us and ran a mile, shrieking and squealing, as girls apparently do, in the opposite direction.

When I was about twelve or thirteen I used to cycle down to Ben Phizaklea's house and we'd play endless hours of Subbuteo table soccer. If you haven't seen it before, Subbuteo is a table soccer game that involves a big sheet of green felt marked out like a football pitch and you use your finger to flick little football figurines, weighed down on half moons of plastic, so that they 'kick' a plastic ball around. If it sounds strange, it was, but we were obsessed: we had teams and league tables and transfer windows and stats and everything. Ben's pitch was better than mine as mine had a stiff, crusted corner where Mam had spilt rice pudding on it, and he also had special goals ('continental', they were marketed as) which allowed us to pretend that we were playing at Manchester City's home ground, Maine Road, which at the time was almost space age in its modernity.

In summer time, after a few games of Subbuteo, we'd head off down the shore to throw rocks at the small community of endangered toads that lived in the tidal ponds, or we'd run up and down the slaggies, the big slag banks left over from the iron smelting industry that towered over the terraces at the southern end of town. The slag was crumbling into scree in parts and if you stood on a pile of rocks you could surf down the slaggie, hundreds of crushed pebbles acting as ball bearings to carry you along. It could end spectacularly badly, but this was the good old days when skin grafts were frowned upon and men smiled warmly at a lad with a compound fracture of the femur.

It was 1975 and it was one of those northern summer evenings that last for ever. Ben and I had tired of Subbuteo and we were mucking about in the narrow croft behind the bus stop, kicking the tops off thistles, or whatever it was that young men did in the days before the Internet. Two lasses from school wandered over, Yvette Tomlinson and Diana Firth. They shouted stuff at us and we shouted stuff back, and then after a while they came over and the four of us mucked about for a bit.

Diana Firth was a good bit shorter than me and had a basin haircut on top of a round face that made her head look like an acorn in the shell. Yvette was like a whippet with lank hair and darting eyes. Ben hooked up with Diana and I started pushing Yvette round and she pushed back; she had brothers and knew how to handle herself. That push and shove soon morphed into a game of chase and, being boys, we were faster and stronger and thought that that made us better at that kind of thing. Ben soon got Diana but I was after Yvette for ages and no matter how hard I chased her she let me catch her in the end, and straight away we fell into a tumbling wrestle with lots of 'tickling' and inducing that kind of hysterical laughter that produces tears and a sore tummy. Except it wasn't really tickling. I don't know if we'd put a name to what we were doing but we ended up flushed and wide-eyed and looking at each other and, when we looked at Ben and Diana, they were looking at us a bit wide-eyed too.

Twenty-five years later I was visiting home and headed down the paper shop. I'd just come out with an *Evening Mail* and a Mars bar when who should I bump into but Yvette Tomlinson and her mam. Yvette was a mother herself now and was dressed a bit like her own mother, but she still had a bloom about her and the pair of us were both instantly back in that field, surrounded by thistles and long grass, flushed and wide-eyed and wondering what we'd just done. I looked at her and she looked at me and we both broke out in the biggest daftest grins and then her mother looked at me and then at Yvette and then back at me and then shook her head and said, 'I don't want to know! I just . . . do *not* want to know!'

* * *

I look a bit odd in this picture because I'm trying to smile without showing a prominent front tooth that stuck out like a gravestone. I had 'crowded teeth' but I didn't get braces; in fact, I didn't even know what tooth braces were until my late teens. The world of dentistry in my neck of the woods was, at that time, still carried out by men on street corners in blood-soaked aprons. In one of my school diaries I have an appointment to go to the school clinic, which was at the end of the school driveway but still on the grounds, next to where the buses turned around. This was where we had immunisations and were checked for ringworm or TB or whatever, and they checked our teeth too. They sent a note home and (as faithfully recorded in my school diary) three days after the first appointment I went to the clinic, had a mask put on me with knock-out gas, and woke up with four less teeth, two from the top set and two from the bottom. I was a bit surprised by the process, but on the up side I did get out of science and RE.

My own children's teeth are gleaming and perfect (as are those of all their friends) because, like all the parents of our children's friends, we poured a year's mortgage payments into the accounts of their orthodontist. I don't begrudge it—I certainly wouldn't want either of them to go through the ongoing dental problems that I've had in life—but the fact that expensive dental work is an accepted rite of passage for my kids and the class of parent that I've become is a stark reminder of just how much things have changed since my own childhood.

Those changes, the ones that take place within a short period of time, are more difficult to reconcile than the big changes. My dad left school at fourteen and worked on a farm, ploughing fields with horse teams. Getting electricity was a big deal for him. And yet that doesn't seem as wild as the changes in paediatric dentistry that have occurred in my lifetime. To say of the near past that 'it was a different time' isn't convincing; just ask any British male celebrity of a certain age confronted with 271 child sex allegations from the early Seventies.

* * *

Subject selection was a simple affair at my secondary school. One morning we boys were trouped out to the top playground and a teacher shouted, 'Those lads that want to do woodwork: stand over by the toilet block. Lads that want to do metalwork: over by the prefabs.' Have you ever seen a gigantic flock of starlings swoop and turn across a winter sky like one huge single organism? We weren't quite like that. We were more like gnus crossing the Serengeti, heads down and moving instinctively, occasionally bumping into one another. Ninety-eight per cent of the boys headed towards the toilet block. I huddled with the smaller pack by the prefabs.

I love wood and wooden things but I'm terrible at doing anything with it. The word I'm looking for is 'affinity': I have no affinity for it. I can admire a perfect dovetail joint or a Japanese temple made with interlocking timbers but I can't even make a fishing tackle box. I'm looking at it now, my second-year woodwork project. It's a poor effort, and that isn't a subjective opinion. It has the authority of my woodwork teacher, who'd seen hundreds of fishing tackle boxes over the years and knew a poor-effort one when he saw it. I can see where I'd started a cut with a tenon saw then realised it was an eighth of an inch out and started again. The same applies to the boat I made: joints that waggle about rather than fit snugly, vertical cuts that drift off at 15 degrees.

My most cack-handed school woodwork project by far was the letter knife we made in first year. I'll bet that most kids wouldn't even know what a letter knife was these days, let alone how to make one. The idea of this task was to introduce us to the surform, a tool that was a file crossed with a cheese grater. We used the surform to gouge and shape large, useful blocks of wood into smaller, less useful blocks of wood. I was over-enthusiastic, or had poor fine motor skills, or both, but the more I worked on the long, tapered blade of my letter knife the more it snapped or broke. It got shorter and I got angrier and it got shorter and I got frustrated and it got shorter to the point where I was left with a carefully formed handle from which the merest nub of a blade protruded. I'm looking at it now and it actually makes me laugh out loud. The saddest thing about it is that when we'd finished it we had to sand it, stain it and lacquer it; all that finessing and finishing off for a piece of wood that sat perfectly in my hand but had no purpose whatsoever, other than perhaps to be a handle for something else.

But back in the playground next to the prefabs, once we'd been divided from the main herd, we in the smaller pack went to the metalwork rooms. Here we were taught by Mr Smith and Mr Allinson. They were brilliant teachers, partly because they loved what they did but mostly because they despised the woodwork boys with their clean, soft hands and dusty aprons. Those of us who'd chosen metalwork were made to feel superior to the other kids in a way that no other teachers ever managed. Selecting history over geography was just a preference; by choosing metalwork over woodwork we'd shown to Mr Smith and Mr Allinson that we'd passed a test of character. Mr Allinson had been a blacksmith. On slow days, while we tried to solder scoops made of metal plate or beat a sheet of copper into a bowl shape he would move towards the forge, fire it up and hammer out magical shapes on the anvil from lengths of steel: a ram's head, a perfect rose in bloom, a twisted and ornate gate decoration. We knew when he'd finished a piece because, without a word, he'd plunge it back into the hottest part of the coals where it would quickly sputter and spark and burst into a ball of metal flames. Then he'd simply head back to his desk, and we'd carry on soldering and beating. We thought he was fantastic.

The cannon was one of my final pieces in what was the equivalent of my Year 10 exams. It's quite complex because I had to use a shaping machine for the carriage and a lathe with a three-jaw chuck for the barrel and a four-jaw chuck for the wheels. I used the borer for the barrel, and then there was the welding and so on.

I was proud of it but at the same time I knew it wasn't all that great. The gun carriage seemed disproportionately big for the actual cannon. I had ambitions to make it into a working cannon and asked Mr Allinson if he thought that it might be possible. To his credit he didn't laugh out loud but considered for a minute (or at least gave the impression of considering) before saying that, on balance, it might not be possible. He said something about not having the proper tools to rifle the inside of the barrel, and also problems with recoil that my carriage wasn't properly designed to accommodate. I nodded, disappointed but ready to accept Mr Allinson's opinion. I'll bet he laughed his head off in the staffroom later.

* * *

My cub scouts cap! There's no neckerchief or woggle but the cap is still there. Our troop's neckerchief was red and green. Some boys had leather woggles but the new kids had fancy plastic ones. It looks tiny, as though it's for a tiny person's head. Which it is: it's for a tiny version of me.

I was never mad for cubs. I can't remember whose idea it was to go, whether I was pushed into it or whether I nagged and nagged to go and then got bored after two weeks but was ordered to keep going by vengeful parents (the most likely version). In summer it was a nice walk down to the prefab building near the sandy lane where the cub troop met. The scoutmaster was Jackie Fallon, who was also the town barber. We did all the cub-type things, getting badges for doing cubby stuff. I thought we'd be lighting fires and swinging from ropes over bottomless canyons but I got one badge for throwing a ball to another cub ten times with my right hand, then catching it with my right hand when he threw it back, then throwing it to him ten times with my left hand, then catching it with my left hand when he threw it back. Even at ten years of age it seemed weak. But there are two standout memories of that time.

Cubs was on a Wednesday night. Depending on the time of year, by the time I walked the mile or so up the hill I'd be home in time for either *Mission Impossible* or *The Man from UNCLE.* If for some reason I'd scraped a few pennies together, or if I'd pinched them out of Mam's purse, I could stop at the Railway Hotel and buy some Fruit Salads or some Black Jacks (eight for a penny) and suck on them on the way up. But one hot summer's night, when I got home, Mam gave me some money and a bag and I went up to the Bay Horse to buy a couple of bottles of brown ale and some lemonade. (Yes, I was still in my cubs uniform. No, I wasn't asked my age.) The thrill of that shandy stayed with me for years, and quite possibly triggered a near-catastrophic thirst for alcohol during my teenage years. But it was worth it.

The other memory was when Colin Thomson went mental with Jackie. I knew two things about Colin: he was a fiery little bugger, and he supported Stoke City. Supporting Stoke City was utterly bewildering. He might as well have been learning to yodel in Sanskrit or perform open-heart surgery. Until Colin came along my benchmark for that kind of madness was Tony Shearon who supported Ipswich Town (yeah, I know), but then it turned out that Tony had some tenuous connection with the place, like having been born there, so I suppose that made it OK.

Anyway, one night we'd had to do something onerous and based on olde worlde Baden Powell stuff like creeping up on other cubs and hitting them with a stick. Colin didn't want to do this. (I think his mam and dad made him go; he wasn't all that keen on anything we did.) Jackie was not used to having to deal with boys with 'attitude'. His haircut for small boys had a trademark style; you could say it was his signature cut. Certainly, all boys for a three-mile radius had the same one. You didn't settle yourself onto the padded board that raised yourself up to mirror level and say, 'I'd like a little off the top, please, Jackie. Bring the sides in and leave the shape at the back as natural as possible.' Bzzzz! Next!

Colin did not have a Jackie Fallon haircut. It was almost to his collar and spoke of rebellion. He would not creep across the ground. He would not crawl up and ambush other cubs. Voices were raised. It became heated. The rest of us cubs shrank back. I had never seen a kid defy a grown-up and it made my world all topsy-turvy. Colin got angrier than I'd ever seen any kid ever get; his face was red, and hot tears of rage poured down his cheeks. And then Jackie Fallon pushed him too far, maybe he used some old school discipline technique that might have worked in the Fifties but this was the Seventies, maybe even 1971, and Colin Thomson shouted 'Fuck off! Fuck off to you and fuck off to your stupid fucking crawling around!' He threw his cap on the floor and ran to the door and gave Jackie one last, screaming '*Fuck off!*' Colin Thomson never came back to cubs.

I can't remember the immediate moments after that, whether we all quietly went back to crawling around or whether Jackie had to do something violent to another more pliant cub in order to reassert his authority. But I was in awe of Colin Thomson. Stoke City went up in my estimation and to this day, whenever I see the football results, I look out for Stoke City and think of Colin Thomson.

* * *

The stuff we made in woodwork and metalwork class was the stuff that lads had made for decades, if not centuries. For example, another practical item we made, to complement our letter knife, was a toasting fork. The fireplace in our house still had the same function as a hearth from a Neanderthal cave; it was where we gathered and burnt things. In winter it was the centre of the universe, a place of warmth and comfort at a time when the toilet—located three and a half miles away at the other end of the hallway—was as cold as Robert Falcon Scott's tent.

Because of its importance in our lives the fireplace had its own equipment, the stuff necessary to keep it running. Our house was new and so it had a 1960 fireplace with tilework in a mixture of different shades of grey. Maybe grey was the new black in 1960 or maybe it was part of the whole austerity Britain vibe that was going down at the time. There was an old hearth rug, pocked by burns from embers that had jumped out from the fire. On one side there was a coalscuttle and a set of tools: a brush, a pan, a poker and a toasting fork. Our little set had been made during his apprenticeship by the now-vanished Uncle Malcolm (last heard of somewhere in South Africa). It was a bright red perspex tube that stood upright on tripod legs, each leg ended in a black plastic ball (just like the stand for Joey the budgie's cage, up in the cock loft). At the top, three arms radiated outwards, and from these hung the brush, pan and fork. The centre of the tube was hollow and acted as a kind of sheath for the poker.

There were three parts to the toasting fork I made in metalwork: a handle, a long stem, and the three-tined fork at the end. Each part was supposed to display some skill or ability to work metal. My handle was made out of a bit of flat bar and was based on some kind of Celtic battle design, or at least a twelve-year-old's understanding of a Celtic battle design. Some of the kids with more imagination and ability made handles out of pieces of coloured perspex threaded onto a rod, like chicken and capsicum on a kebab skewer, then turned on a lathe to make a multicoloured handle. To make the stem part it had to be heated in the forge before being hammered flat and twisted to create an ornamental centrepiece. The fork part was made out of flat metal, with the tines scribed out and cut with a hacksaw before being filed to the correct shape.

My tines were not particularly fine; in fact, they were so wide and fat that any attempt to pierce a slice of bread with them ended up with the bread being shredded till just the crust was left. When we used it, the night I brought it home, we ended up just laying the slice of bread on top of the fork part and toasting it that way, or at least until the handle became too hot to hold. I don't think we ever used it again but it did sit proudly next to Malcolm's hearth-fettling equipment for a good couple of weeks.

* * *

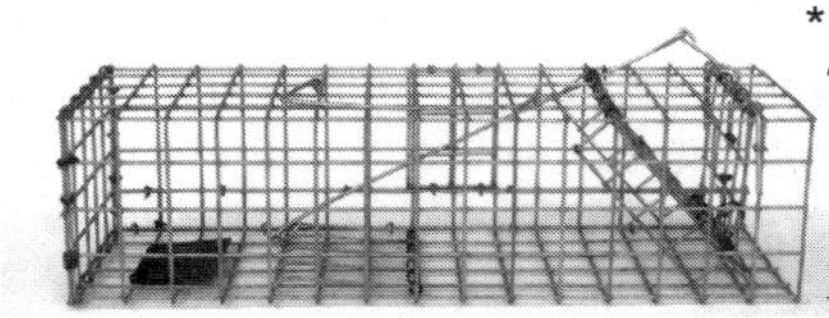

The people who work for the Australian Quarantine and Inspection Service must see the vague term 'household goods' a million times on the labels of the boxes that flood daily into the country from hither and yonder. 'Household goods' covers all kinds of objects, from the battered frying pan to the three-kilo block of cocaine. In my case I used it to describe the rat-trap that Dad insisted I take home, and which I pulled out of Box 1. It has nothing to do with my childhood, though shooting vermin certainly did.

The summer before the holiday we had at Dad's place, the one where I packed up the five boxes, had been ideal for rats. I don't know how he found out about this brand of rat-trap but it was of such a cunning and unbeatable design that he bought three of them: one for himself, one for my brother-in-law and one for me to take home to Australia. Every time I try to set it I have to remember how the door opens and how the bit of wire loops back to the little pad that the rat stands on to trigger the door to shut behind it. I haven't caught any rats with it yet, though my brother-in-law's single-handedly crushing his local rodent population. When I talk to Dad on the phone on a Sunday it's one of the questions he'll ask me, whether I've caught a rat yet, and when I say no there's a brief silence where, once over, he'd have made that 'Pfft' sound.

Dad likes to see us off with useful gifts. After a holiday a few years back, when the kids were little, he gave each of them a couple of foxes' tails—big red white-tipped brushes—to play with on the journey home. It is indeed a very long journey from Cumbria to New South Wales and this was in the days before aeroplane seats had screens in the backs of headrests with Tetris and twenty-six channels of kids' shows on them. So, hey, a couple of brushes. That'll keep them quiet for hours. 'Take these to Australia, kids!' he said and the kids waved the foxes' tails around in big looping circles, one in each hand, ran up and down the hallway where once I'd bombed toy soldiers with golf balls, and they shouted 'Yay!' and Dad pretended to be a foxhound and chased them around, barking and pretending to catch them and tear their faces off. Good old Granddad!

I told Dad about Customs and about the Australian Quarantine and Inspection Service, about how a man in a uniform would board the aircraft and spray Mortein over the startled passengers. I told him about the documentaries popular on Australian telly that are set in the Customs part of airports, about the scared, feckless or shame-faced smugglers of drugs and homemade Fijian fish soup who get caught every week, and of course the sniffer beagles, the adorable stars of the show who gambol around the luggage carousel before suddenly stopping to sit down next to a suitcase, staring up with those gorgeous brown eyes at some sweat-stained drug mule. That'll be me, I said. Those beagles, they don't miss a trick. To which Dad replied, 'Be buggered. Take 'em, kids.' Yay, Granddad!

It wasn't worth the argument, not when we were ten minutes away from starting the long, long journey home. I'll chuck them in the bin at Preston station, I thought.

Unfortunately, the kids became perversely attached to these brushes. I managed to distract them with sugary food and hid the brushes in the big suitcase, hoping that in the excitement of the journey they'd forget about them. It worked really well; in fact, it worked so well that I only remembered what I'd done when we were disembarking in Sydney and walking towards luggage carousel number three. Which is when I saw the adorable prancing and gambolling of the beagle.

I don't think my stomach has ever sunk so far so quickly. The line *Did you pack the contents of this case yourself, sir?* never sounded so ominous. The carousel jolted into action and the bags popped out of the chute like eggs laid by a gigantic hidden insect. The kids' cases came out first and I smiled a wan smile at the beagle, in his cute little AQIS hi-viz jacket, as he frolicked up and down and between us.

The big bag took an age to arrive but eventually it thudded onto the scallop-shaped tiles. I hauled it off and, with what was meant to be an air of detached insouciance, I breezed towards the green gateway. Of course there was a queue and of course the beagle was directed away from the carousel and towards the lines of people trying to shuffle out and into the freedom of arrivals. I could see him, mister adorable in his doggie hi-viz, zigzagging towards us. I must have had a complexion the colour of window putty but suddenly a break opened up and, grabbing kids and cases in one massive bundle, surged towards the opening. I didn't dare to at first but, as I rounded the ramp in front of the crowds of waiting friends and relatives I peeked back at the queue. The beagle was there, staring at me, his eyes narrowed, his nose raised and a look of intense concentration on his face. He knew that smell from somewhere. Was it hash? Was it a lovely big ball of something resinous? Was it plastic explosive? It's . . . it's . . . *that's* what it is!

Too late, puppy dog.

* * *

Dad was always the first up in the morning and he usually cleared out the ashes from the grate and set a fire up with paper and kindling so that it'd be ready for Mam to put a match to when she came home from work. There's a peculiar muffled sound that a shovel makes when it digs into a grate full of soft ashes. He'd bring lengths of tongue and groove home from the building sites and chop this for kindling. Out in the garage he would cut the planks crossways with a bow saw, stand them on their edges and chop them down the grain into perfect lengths with an axe. I always wanted to do it but he wouldn't let me because he knew that I'd chop my fingers off trying, but I think he also knew that when he went to work I was out there having a go. I could never match the measured rhythm he worked at, whether it was laying bricks or mixing mortar or chopping kindling.

After a while I took on the role of setting the fire. I love watching a flame take hold. It's mesmerising, like watching the dot disappear on the TV screen when you turn it off at night, or watching lard melt in a chip pan. If the fire wouldn't draw you got a couple of sheets of the *News of the World*, the biggest paper ever, and held it across the hearth to create a draft. Sometimes the fire would catch with a dull *woomp!* and if you left it there too long the flames would cause the newspaper to become brown and brittle. This was a treatment that was also useful when making treasure maps you'd drawn look ancient and valuable.

We have a gas fire now, as does Dad. It's very efficient and it's better for the environment but, like everything that is an improvement on the original (skim milk versus proper milk, olive oil margarine versus butter, electric cars versus real cars) it is actually rubbish. This is the evolution of things: good, better, best, rubbish.

* * *

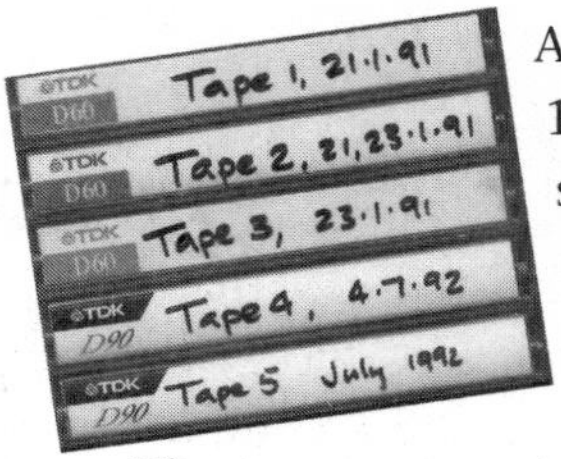

A couple of tape cassettes, from January 1991. This is from long after I left home so I must have made them one holiday and left them behind, and they've gotten chucked in with the rest of my stuff.

The tapes are part of a series of recordings I made with my grandparents, Tom and Sally, over several years. Tom and Sally adopted Norma during the war after she was evacuated from her home in Salford. They were reluctant to be taped at first but, once they'd got into the swing of it, couldn't be stopped. There's a pattern to them with Grandad Tom—the original cantankerous old git from central casting—dominating proceedings in his flat Northern baritone until some key fact of the story is necessary. At this point he falters and makes an imperious clucking sound and Nanna Sally, the brains of the outfit who sat at his side, quietly provides the critical information. At which point Tom immediately resumes. The one time Sally does get to speak is when she talks about the grammar school scholarship that got her off the farm; sadly, economic circumstances meant that she had to give the scholarship up. This part of the transcript sums up everything about the two of them:

Mark: You enjoyed school, didn't you, Nanna?
Sally: Aye, I did that.
Tom: Pffft.
Mark: How come you didn't go any further? Did you have to go back to the farm?
Sally: Service. I went into service.
Mark: What, like a maid?

Sally: Aye! Blackin' fires and scrubbin' floors. I could have had a higher education.
Tom: Higher education? Higher bloody rubbish!
Sally: Hmm.

Genealogy had been an interest of mine for as long as I could remember, though it was a while before I summoned up the courage to put a tape recorder on the table and get them to talk. It was all a bit anoraky in the 1970s and 80s—musty libraries and reels of microfiche—but now there are adverts on telly for ancestry dot com and the show *Who Do You Think You Are?* is syndicated around the world. I love watching that show, even if it's the South African version with people I've never heard of. The people they feature are celebrities: actors or sportsmen or people in the public spotlight. There's always a bit at the start of the show where they set the scene, with the celebrity confessing that they know nothing about their family (which always makes me gasp with incredulity: how could you not be interested?), then the celebrity goes back to the family home, often a modest detached house with a nice garden. And here's the point of difference that sets them apart from me, that defines them as celebrities: they go up to the front door *and knock*. One of their parents will answer the door (another point of difference: the parents are always so healthy and presentable) but the thing that bewilders me the most is that *they use the front door* and *they knock*.

It was years before I remember using our front door. And as for knocking? The procedure was that you went round the back of someone's house and shouted, 'Is Martin playing out?' Even adults used the back door. On Friday Pat Corrigan came round with the flatties he'd caught in the estuary and we'd get a few for tea, then the next visitor was Reg Pine from the Co-op who'd pick up the insurance money Mam left on the kitchen counter with the insurance book. I'm not sure what we were being insured against, I just knew that it was Reg getting the insurance money. If we were sitting in the front room watching telly or eating our tea then Reg would shout through so we knew he'd been and one of us (usually Dad) would shout back, 'Righto, Reg!' Front door? Key?

I knew that there were front-door-users out there in the world because I saw them on telly but I wasn't really sure if they *really* existed, as in real life. They were the people we knew to be posh, and it wasn't just the wearing of suits, working in offices and having a snifter before dinner that showed you to be posh. It was using the front door and using a key to get in.

There were other things that posh people did. Posh people cut sandwiches into triangles instead of oblongs. They had 'lunch' at dinner time and 'dinner' at tea time. They called cooking foil 'aluminium foil' or 'silver foil' instead of its proper name, which is 'tin foil'. They had the phone on. Their kids knew how to talk to grown-ups. They were scared of ferrets.

My type used the back door, which was always unlocked. I had breakfast then dinner then tea then a bit of supper. You had to be careful what you had for supper because some foods make you dream. The worst for this was cheese on toast, and bananas. I'm all right about eating cheese late at night now, but only a fool would eat a banana after seven o'clock. If I asked for cheese on toast our mam or dad would shake their head and say, in a voice, 'You'll only dream!' or 'You'll have dreams!' in the same way you might say to someone about to jump off a waterfall and into a tiny pool, 'You'll end up in a wheelchair!' Aye, dreams: you don't want to be having them.

These were the things that I used to know defined posh folk. How could I ever have known that, one day, I would eat bananas at all hours of the night and cut my sandwiches into triangles? But I still don't use the front door.

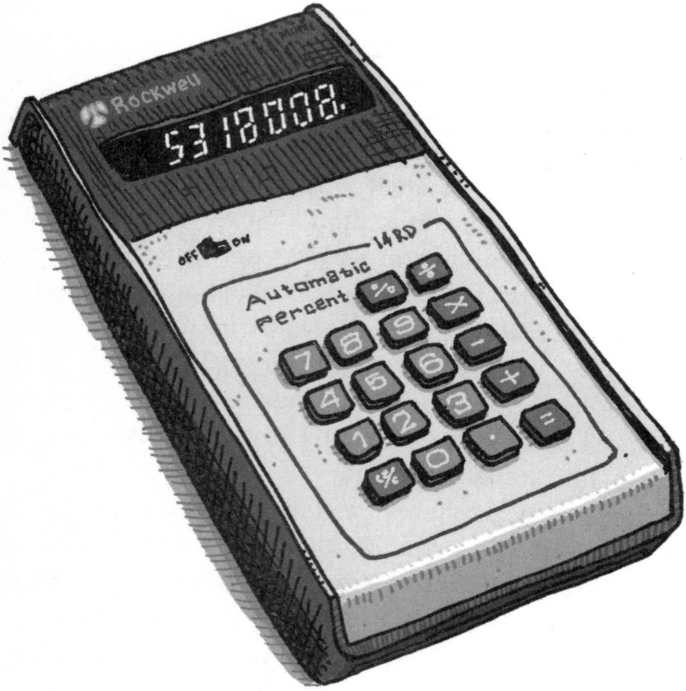

Rockwell
OFF ON
14RD
Automatic
Percent

Box 2

Around the time that I learned that 'rectangle' was the grown-up word for 'oblong' I became aware that not everyone said 'our mam': they said 'my mum'. And at school I also learned that 'take away' was really 'minus', 'multiply' was the proper way to say 'times' and 'divide' was the same as 'share'. But 'add' was always 'add'.

This calculator can add, take away, times and share. And it can do something with percentages, as indicated by the chunky square-shaped button with a % sign on it. Archaeologists of the future will call the 1980s 'the Great Fingertip Shift'. Before this time all buttons were huge but then, at some point, a person in a laboratory worked out that you could squeeze an entire keyboard onto a space the size of a matchbox. It was after this time that people with fat fingertips started dying out, eventually becoming extinct in 2197.

The first calculator that I saw was owned by Tony Oldcorn. The Oldcorns also had the phone on, a red one like Commissioner Gordon's off *Batman*. The way to school was up a muddy lane behind Dickie Taylor's chicken sheds but, if it was too wet, we'd go up the main road with its long sweeping bend by the pub with a high wall with no pavement and if a slate truck went past then you might have to press yourself into the wall a bit to avoid being clipped by a wing mirror.

Tony's parents were sensible about road safety. He was in the Tufty Club (a road safety awareness campaign that was headed, inexplicably, by a squirrel called Tufty) and he had a diddy jacket, a kind of fluorescent safety vest that made his small body more visible to the weary care-worn drivers of slate trucks. My parents were no slouches on the road safety front either and I had a reflective white armband that I wore on my right arm going up the hill and left arm coming down. My cousin from over the field had an armband just like mine. (I can imagine my dad and his brother looking at the price of a pair of armbands, looking at one another and coming to a silent agreement. *Both* arms? Pfft.)

On those wet mornings we'd gather in Tony's front hall on the way to school. If there were a couple of minutes to wait while Tony was wrangled into his diddy jacket the rest of us would stare at the red telephone, willing it to ring.

I like the colours of my calculator's plastic. The Seventies always get laughed off as 'the decade that fashion forgot' and if films or TV shows are set in those days then everyone has brown cords and purple nylon body shirts and the carpets have orange swirly patterns. This calculator has nice shades of what modern paint makers would describe as caramel, walnut and pumice; that is, brown and grey.

I compare it to the calculator on my smart phone. It's a testament to the early calculator's design team that the phone's calculator layout is almost exactly the same as the old Rockwell 14RD. The major drawback of the modern calculator, however, is the rounded numbering system, which makes it impossible to write upside-down words such as *HELLO* and *BOOBIES*. Another olde tymes joy denied to the needle-fingertipped kids of today.

* * *

There comes a point in your life when you say something like, 'That car is black' and someone else—maybe someone a bit older or more worldly wise—says, 'There is no such colour as black. There are only shades of grey.' And if you're really unlucky they may have had some art training and be able to tell you in detailed length why this is so.

I'm looking at my schoolbooks and, for the most part, they're full of dull stuff: badly coloured maps of Europe at the outbreak

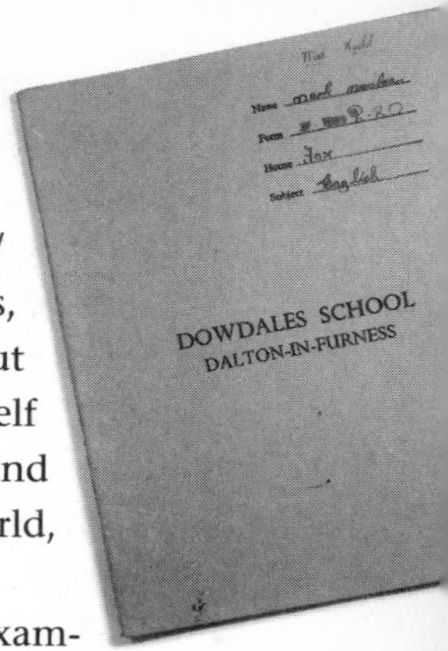

of the Great War; lists of French vocabulary items; tables of comparatives and superlatives (in which I've written 'tall / taller / tallest'; 'late / later / latest'; 'bad / badder / baddest'); more lists, this time of the books of the Old Testament. But occasionally a piece jumps out at me and I see a self who saw a world free from tones and shades and hues. Only two colours were needed in this world, and black and white did the job very well.

My teenage approach to old age is a classic example of black-and-whiteness. Nearly all the boyfriends of the girls in my year were at least two years older than me. Some of these boyfriends had even left school, and would roll up to the bus stop in their swanky Hillman Imps and Mini Clubmans to pick these girls up. As for people in their twenties, well, there was really no difference between them and the rows of slack-jawed dotards parked in front of nursing home televisions and smelling of wee.

I'm looking at an English book from 1974. We'd been given a descriptive piece to write and I'd done mine about hanging around the arcades at Blackpool pleasure beach, watching the sliders on the penny fountains push back and forth while people try to slide coins down the races and into positions where, in their dreams, mountains of brown pennies, silver shillings and brass threepenny bits cascade down the chutes and into the burnished, bowl-shaped cups below. There were other machines there, the one-armed bandits and the shooting gallery that was like a submarine's periscope, with a button to launch torpedoes against unsuspecting ships. When you'd blown your dough on the penny fountains, the fruit machines and the torpedoes you could get notes changed at a counter with a perspex front. In my story someone has to change a pound note and the woman behind the counter I describe as a 'withered hag', so in my mind she may have been in her mid twenties.

In another story we were given the subject 'Alone' and I wrote about being at home alone at night and waiting for Mam and Dad to get back from the pub. Teachers reading such a story these days would be obliged under mandatory reporting requirements to alert Social Services, but in the story I describe my relief as I hear a car door slam followed by the familiar sound of my mother's 'manic cackling'. Because that's how old women laugh, isn't it?

I recently read a friend's daughter's descriptive piece in which she wrote of being on a rooftop overlooking the city and watching the people walking around the mall below her at lunchtime. She describes the people as 'milling around like mindless zombies', once again because that's what old people do. (For 'old people', read 'anyone who's left school'.) Old people no longer have any sense of purpose, they simply stagger about occasionally bumping into one another or into lampposts, clearly with no conscious thought process. And it's because they are *old*.

The irony is that teenagers are the ones with no idea of what they're doing or where they're going and it's only us withered hags, cackling maniacally as our eyes alight on the Grim Reaper's scythe, who haven't got time to waste in stumbling around bumping into another. We've got stuff to do! Blogs to post! Entire box sets of *Breaking Bad* to get through!

* * *

I've always had a bit of a thing for tin boxes; I can't throw them away even though the only thing they're useful for is the thing that they contained, but no longer contain. Sometimes I try to find new uses for them by storing odd buttons or other bits of useless stuff that will never ever get used and should be chucked out.

The exception to this rule about tins and usefulness is Golden Virginia tobacco tins. A quarter ounce of Golden

Virginia was the birthday and Christmas present of choice for Dad. Me and my sister would sometimes go in together and get a half ounce from Gibson Constable's corner shop. Half ounces came in tins and I've still got a dozen of them in the shed, filled with allen keys, electrical terminals, screw bits for the electric drill and so on.

There is something inexplicably satisfying about opening and closing the lid of a tobacco tin: hold the base in one hand, put your thumb under the corner of the lid and turn and . . . pop. I love the sound and feel of parts machined to a high tolerance when they click together with a perfect *tchuck!*: the barrel of a shotgun folding into its stock, the click of an ink cartridge as you press it into its slot in the printer carriage, a right-sized ring spanner slipping onto a nut.

* * *

Mam wasn't much of a cook, but these are the things she did best:

1. Fried Spam, chips and processed peas. I can't remember if 'processed peas' are an actual thing or something I just made up. (I just looked them up on the Tesco website: they are real and they still exist.)

2. Shepherd's pie. Here's a thing I didn't know until I was a grown-up. Shepherd's pie is supposed to be a Monday tradition, made with the minced leftover lamb from Sunday's roast. Even though we lived in Cumbria, and for every Cumbrian person there are 26 million sheep, we didn't ever have lamb roast as it was considered too expensive. I do not know where all the sheep went when they left Cumbria. Our Sunday protein of choice was chicken, which was quite a deal. Shepherd's pie was a Thursday dish, served with baked beans, and it just had 'mince' in it, the pink kind that came from some animal that wasn't a sheep.

3. Taty hash. This was one our Mam could cobble together during her dinnertime break. She'd bolt up the hill from the

shoe factory, get a taty hash fettled in a pyrex dish, put it on a low heat and bolt back down for afternoon shift. She must have been fit as a fiddle! I used to hate the smell of taty hash filling the house when I got home from school but I did eat a lot of it, usually with red cabbage and pickled onions.

4. Fish fingers, chips and peas. Oh yeah.

5. Gammon, new potatoes and peas. This was the dish that truly marked the arrival of spring in our house: new spuds and a thick, pink slab of gammon. When The Wife first came over to England she made dinner one night and got some gammon steaks. And she put an Australian twist on it, garnishing each portion of meat with a pineapple ring. We still laugh at the look of distressed horror on Mam and Dad's faces when she served them up.

* * *

I'd forgotten how mad for soccer I was. There's a big deal in Australia about not calling soccer 'soccer' but calling it football, its proper name. I think we used both terms interchangeably, with 'rugby' being for union and 'league' for the thirteen-man game. And I was watching the film *Saturday Night and Sunday Morning* and I'm sure that, at the end, Albert Finney says 'soccer'. So there.

These cards are from Shredded Wheat cereal packets. Breakfast in our house was always a bit of a grab-your-own affair; Dad would be up and gone by the time I crawled out of bed and Mam started work at eight. I didn't like Shredded Wheat but I must have mithered after it till Mam caved in and bought some; I'll bet I pulled the box open, got the card then threw the Shredded Wheat out for the birds. There are three cards, equalling three boxes, by which time I must have got sick of Shredded Wheat or she latched onto what I was doing with it.

And what a swiz: one card with Mick Channon and two—two!—with boring old Colin Todd. What are the chances of that?

Much better were the fixture guides the *Sun* gave away. You collected tokens over a series of days and sent in a postal order and a stamped self-addressed envelope. My love of English football coincided with a catastrophic slump in the national team's fortunes. I barely remember the 1966 World Cup but the 1970 one's burnt into my brain for that come-from-behind win by West Germany in the quarter final. Which Dad thought was hilarious, and he goaded me about it from 1970 to 1979.

There was a big push in the lead-up to the 1970 World Cup in Mexico to rent colour tellies. Britain's independent broadcasters were at the time a patchwork of small companies like Anglia down south, Border up north and Cymru in Wales. Our one was Granada and, as well as broadcasting, they rented tellies. I can still sing their catch cry: 'It's great service you get / Renting your TV set / Frrrrrom Granada!'

The Germans rolled us at Mexico and that seemed to set the tone for a decline that lasted most of my youth, certainly from the age of eight to eighteen. The *Sun* soccer book has a feature article on Gerd 'Der Bomber' Muller, the Bayern Munich star who scored the winner against us in Mexico. There's also a list of the 'Big transfers of 1973/74', with Bob Latchford—a strapping, barrel-chested centre forward—moving from Birmingham City to Everton for an eye-watering £350,000 (about a week's wage for a modern Premier League player). But, without being too disrespectful to Bob Latchford, I'll bet that he didn't strike fear into German hearts in the way that Der Bomber struck fear into my little English one. I wonder what damage was done to my psyche by those seemingly endless defeats that I remember in those years; that Domarski goal for Poland at Wembley that put us out at the group stages in 1973, or the 2.1 defeat against Norway in the lead-up to the '82 World Cup? This kind of thing can do irreparable damage to a little lad's mind.

As well as talking about football and collecting cards I also played it. The field over the road from our house, the croft, has a slope of about 60 degrees. There's a row of posts for washing lines at the top and these served as goalposts for a variety of games with elaborate rules, depending on how many people had turned up to play. If there weren't enough people to have proper sides you could have a French goalie, which was someone who was nominated and who could turn from an outfield player to goalie when they were in the penalty area. There were games like Wembley and Workington, which rotated sides as goals were scored or corners and goal kicks accrued.

But regardless of whatever game was being played the One Rule that Bound Them All was this: if the ball went bouncing down the hill and into the vast jungle of Scotch thistles at the bottom it was the job of the last person who touched it to go and get it. I reckon that this rule developed in me an ability to nick a ball into someone for a perfect rebound, a skill you just can't replicate in ordinary training drills. As skills go it hasn't been the most useful one in my adult life and it sums up what was wrong with 1970s English football. We'd gone from hoofing in 30-yard screamers like Bobby Charlton to tippy-toe little defensive kicks to avoid ending up in the thistles. My footballing development had been stifled. I blame Der Bomber.

* * *

Knowing man things is getting harder. I lift the bonnet of my car and it's like someone's stolen the engine and put a black plastic suitcase in its place. There are a few funnels for fluids to be poured into but, to be honest, I don't even do that. Every 10,000 kilometres I take it to a man who does know what to do and he does all the adjusting and fluid topping-up, and I

thank him and put my soft uncalloused editor's hands into my pocket, pull out my wallet and give him money.

There are many things that a man feels he must know. Some are practical (how to trace an electrical fault, how to change a tyre, how to start a whipper-snipper on the first go) and others are drawn from the world of the fanciful (how to land a plane when the pilot's collapsed, how to skin a bear, how to do that thing with the two-up thing on Anzac Day).

Most men lead quiet and unassuming lives. On those occasions when men find themselves in desperate situations—a hostage crisis or a hijacking—we other men, watching it unfold from the comfort of our lounge chairs, are forced to examine ourselves and ask the dread question: What would I do? We like to think that we'd take out the gunman or storm the cockpit (and then, to the cheers and adulation of the tearful passengers, land the jet) but I'm willing to bet that many would learn to live with the guilt, shame and humiliation that follow survival.

Which is a darkly introspective way to arrive at my cycling proficiency test. I don't think they do it anymore, which is a Bad Thing. There was an organisation called RoSPA—the Royal Society for the Prevention of Accidents—and it administered the tests and produced these rather lovely leaflets. I think we should have RoSPA again. What a good idea! An actual Royal Society to take care of uneven pavements, and mugs of hot tea thoughtlessly placed too close to keyboards.

I was about ten when I took my cycling proficiency test. It's a marker of the nerd that I was that I not only hung onto the leaflets, but also the appointment card and the examiner's score sheet.

I did quite well on 'Starting and turning right' and 'Braking (emergency), stopping and parking' and got full marks on

'Highway Code and other questions', but I performed less well on 'Riding position, pedalling, and cycle control'. I dropped points on 'From a standstill ride slowly between two straight lines 75 feet long and 2 feet wide without touching the lines either side' and 'Pedalling action: Soles of the feet alternately pushing forward and downward on pedals with a good ankling movement'. The examiner did not miss a trick, and I have to admit that poor ankling movement has dogged me throughout my entire life.

The leaflets have charming graphics in two-colour themes: puce and sky blue for 'Pedalling and Braking'; lime green and French blue for 'Starting and Stopping'; and purple mixed with a robust orange for 'Turning Right and Left'. The boys and girls in the illustrations are all smartly dressed (the girls in hats and blazers). I'm put in mind of a world when our obedience as children was assumed, even if this wasn't our reality. 'Turning Right' must have been important because it gets its own two-page spread. Perhaps it's because 'The skilful cyclist turns right or left with great care, especially at road junctions not controlled by traffic lights or police'. I have an image now of a Ladybird book with a stern-looking but avuncular English bobby holding up a white gauntlet and pausing a line of post-war Austins and Morrises so that a respectful and smartly blazered young lady can Turn Right.

'The procedure for turning right described in this leaflet must in no circumstances be carried out at night if your lights are poor, or if they go out when you stop. This applies particularly to users of dynamo sets.' Dynamo sets!

There are some things, like dynamos and magnetos, that I feel I should know about, but don't. This is man knowledge. There was a lad called Shaun Carroll who had a dynamo on his bike and when he rode down the hill near our house at top speed his front light was as bright as a motorbike's. In winter he wore clogs with steel segs in and when he came down his clogs, trailing on the tarmac, sent out showers of sparks behind him.

It was spectacular, but to this day I don't know what a dynamo actually is, or how it works, or how it's different to a magneto. Or what a magneto is, and how it works. Every man has a weak spot in his man knowledge; we all have something that we feel we—as men—should know, but don't. This is mine, and I feel somehow a little bit less of a man for not knowing.

* * *

The Sixties and Seventies were the golden age of the hobby. There was always a book full of lists in which young men could record sightings of things and then tick them off, or albums in which they could stick things. I had a stamp album. This wasn't uncommon; in fact, it's a little known fact that all boys born in Britain after the war were issued with a stamp album at birth.

These soccer stamps are part of the exciting new world that was 1972. We'd just been to the moon and back, and Mars was the obvious next step. It was fair to think that we'd have lunar colonies by 1975, or 1976 at the latest. A friend's dad was an engineer and the firm he worked at built a hovercraft, which he'd flit about the estuary on at weekends when the tide was out. The prefix 'hover' could be added to anything in the early Seventies and somehow make the impossible seem possible.

The *Sun* made these soccer stamps and I liked them because they had real photographs in bright colours. The Royal Mail preferred to use classic paintings and illustrations for its stamps, and while those blocky designs are now considered to be classics to me they looked dated and part of the pre-hover olden days.

The men on the soccer stamps don't look young, even now, and it's hard to believe that they represented the glamorous new world of protein pills and space travel. Where are you now, Brian Harris of Newport County, Eric Winstanley of Barnsley, Brian Godfrey of Bristol Rovers? Was this the high watermark in your career? It would have been for me.

There is no soccer stamp for my local team, the mighty Barrow AFC, because that's the year we were kicked out of the league, never to return. As if it wasn't bad enough having a useless England team, we went from playing in heady fixtures in Division 4 against the likes of Grimsby Town and Workington to the lowly Northern Premier League, where wet Saturdays found us up against other down-and-outs like Matlock Town and Skelmersdale United.

* * *

The Young Ornithologists' Club was the junior version of the RSPB—the Royal Society for the Protection of Birds. I was in the YOC for quite a few years. I would get their boy-friendly magazine (I think we can safely assume that it's membership was entirely male) and I kept lists of birds sighted and I went on sponsored bird-watches to raise funds for whatever it was they did at YOC HQ. I have a letter from Robert Dougal, the grandfatherly old codger who read the news on the BBC and was the YOC's patron, thanking me for the £2.70p I raised by dragging my sorry arse around the sandhills of Drigg one rainy afternoon ticking off birds on a sheet of wet paper.

There's something fustily British about the YOC; even that possessive apostrophe in the title. I can imagine their head office, a brown affair above a newsagent in Bromley. There'd be a kettle and a biscuit roster. A threadbare lino floor and a 60-watt globe dangling from a cloth-insulated length of flex. But at some point they must have 'got with it', hence the funky typesetting on this brochure. The 'oo' of 'look' is actually die cut into the page so that, when you open it, you realise that it's like a pair of binoculars viewing the Arctic tern! Whoa!

It turns out that the YOC did have girl members. I learned this because on the back of the brochure there's a picture of Bobby Charlton (who looked like someone's grandad even when he was firing in screamers for England), and his daughter is a YOC member! Yeah! And there's also a tagline from Susan Stranks, that sexy lass off children's TV show *Magpie*. Turns out I wasn't such a nerdy loser after all!

* * *

Looking at my schoolbooks I'm surprised to find that I wasn't as bad a scholar as I remember having been. Most of the books are filled with the regular, mind-numbingly dull stuff of daily instruction but other parts are quite interesting. The bit in my RE books from 1974 and 1975 on the development of the books that became the Bible was well worth re-reading and I actually learnt a bit, this time round. If only I'd paid a bit more attention at the time. And I also wish they told us something interesting and maybe a bit weird about Ezekiel or Job instead of making us remember endless lists: Joshua, Judges, Ruth, 1 Samuel, 2 Samuel, 1 Kings, 2 Kings.

Girls' names are scrawled in their handwriting on some pages, there are stupid messages between us. That was all part of that thing where you'd nick someone's book and write fake lovey-dovey stuff in it, the 1970s equivalent of finding someone's laptop open and helpfully updating their Facebook status. If boys got hold of your book it was a different story, usually a gigantic knob and balls across the page.

The old knob and balls is amazingly durable as a graffito. I saw an exhibition at Hadrian's Wall with excavations of the soldiers' latrine and there they were, just like my schoolbooks. There's a certain art to it: a few, but not too many, hairs on the balls, and the optional spurts out the end of the knob. I was teaching at a school in Lake Macquarie recently and was rifling through the department's books on Australian history as part of a lesson preparation. There, on the page with an engraving of an early settler using a stump-jump plough, was the most monstrous cock and balls thrusting forth from the battler's trousers. It made me snigger in a schoolboy way but it was also quite comforting to know that, in the age of the smart phone and social media, some things will always be with us.

* * *

This is a poem that I wrote on the fifth of May 1975:

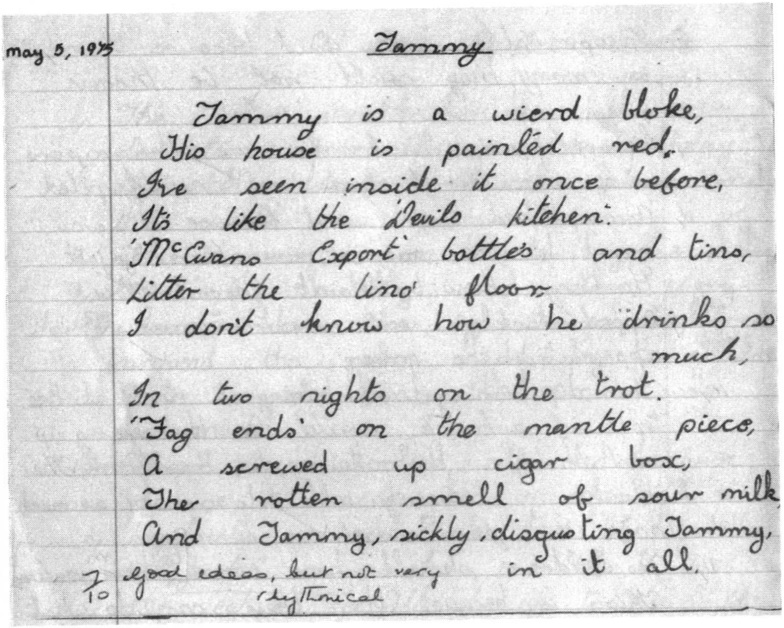

May 5, 1975

Tammy

Tammy is a wierd bloke,
His house is painted red.
I've seen inside it once before,
It's like the Devils kitchen:
'McEwans Export' bottles and tins,
Litter the lino' floor.
I don't know how he drinks so much,
In two nights on the trot.
'Fag ends' on the mantle piece,
A screwed up cigar box,
The rotten smell of sour milk
And Tammy, sickly, disgusting Tammy,
in it all.

7/10 Good ideas, but not very rhythmical

Teacher's comment: '7/10 Good ideas, but not very rhythmical.'

* * *

There was a thing once for penfriends. I'll bet it was thought up by some Esperanto-speaking teacher with too much time on their hands and an optimistic view of a world in which we're all connected and there'll be no more war. If they'd waited a bit longer the Internet would have taken care of that and saved me the torture of having to write all those letters.

The first penfriend I had was in primary school. Our head teacher got the names of the kids in the school up the road from us, at Coniston, and we wrote to them and then they wrote back. Thankfully, after only one letter, it stopped. I think we (kids and teacher) silently agreed that it was too much like hard work.

But then, at secondary school, some bright spark started it up again. I ended up with a letter from a French lass, and the burdensome realisation that I'd have to reply. We did this back and forth a few times and then, out of the blue, came a letter from another French lass. I certainly hadn't asked for that but, being the conscientious young man that I was, I wrote back. But then a letter with a Turkish stamp! And, what's more, the Turkish girl puts, in the PS, that she hadn't actually asked for another penfriend. The same with the incomprehensible letter from the Portuguese girl who wrote (and the words in brackets are in the original), 'I am student. I'm gold coin (more than the people here), told (more than the girls here).' I tried to think of the English word she was looking for that led her to 'gold coin' in her dictionary: medal? sovereign? But, more importantly, who was sending out the names and addresses of European schoolchildren to each other? And why?

Still, duty is duty. I haven't got any of the letters I sent, of course, but seeing this pile of red-and-blue bordered aerogrammes and *par avion*-stickered envelopes took me back to Sunday mornings, sucking the end of a biro and trying to think of something to say about life in rural Cumbria that would make sense to a girl with limited English who lived in Ankara or Porto or on a chicken farm in Brittany.

Given the replies I must have done better than I thought. Florence thanks me for the plan of my house, and in return draws a plan of hers, and Marylene replies with a copy of her school timetable. We exchange stamps, and I always got a top response if I sent them English sweets.

I can see some kind of relationship forming as the letters progress over time. We talk music: 'I have got a tape recorder too' says Jeanine:

> *I don't know 'Yes' but I know the 2 others you talk of. My favourite singer is Patrick Juvet. A lot of people don't like him because he looks like a girl but his songs are very beautiful (according to me).*

We even start to moan at one another: 'My marks in Maths are better than my marks in Spain,' writes Anni. 'I hate Spain and the teacher so, like you hate the Physics.' And a lovely nark-back from Marylene: *'Ton francais n'est pas trop mauvais; il ne faut pas se plaindre'* ('Your French isn't too bad; quit whining to me'!).

It was a good way for a fifteen-year-old boy to understand that what was obvious in one world was not necessarily obvious in another. Given the responses, some of my letters to them must have been as bewildering as theirs were to me. From Lilia Ana in Porto: 'Do you leave very far of London? I went there with seven friends. We amused our self very much. What is the Young Ornithologist Club?' All these baffled schoolchildren writing garbled letters to each other in different languages. Was it supposed to create a harmonious Europe? Well, look at the bloody mess it's in. Forget Nigel Farage and the GFC and the Common Market. I blame penfriends.

* * *

Teaching is a tough profession. People I know who started teaching in the 1970s describe a huge change in attitudes from the public towards the profession; and of course from the students and their parents towards teachers. Teaching was once seen as a fine career, particularly for young women, in the same mould as nursing, social work and other acts of public good. Teachers I've spoken to describe modern graduates as having taken the teaching degree because they couldn't get into architecture or speech pathology, and as seeing teaching as a holding-pattern job where they can earn a decent living until something better comes along. As for the attitudes of students and their parents, well, there are entire libraries devoted to that.

But—apart from the politicisation of the curriculum, the 'all rights, no responsibility' attitude of some kids and parents, and the 'everything in triplicate' approach to health and safety—the thing that really causes a teacher's eyes to narrow and body temperature to soar is not being allowed to tell it how it is, but instead having to provide unique and supportive and representative (but non-judgemental) descriptions of each child's progress within the stringent bureaucratic language of the department's computerised reporting system.

That teacher's comment at the end of my *Tammy* poem, 'Good ideas, but not very rhythmical', was an encouraging moment for me. I didn't always get it right, and other teachers were allowed to be blunt, honest and to the point if my work didn't meet the standards they demanded.

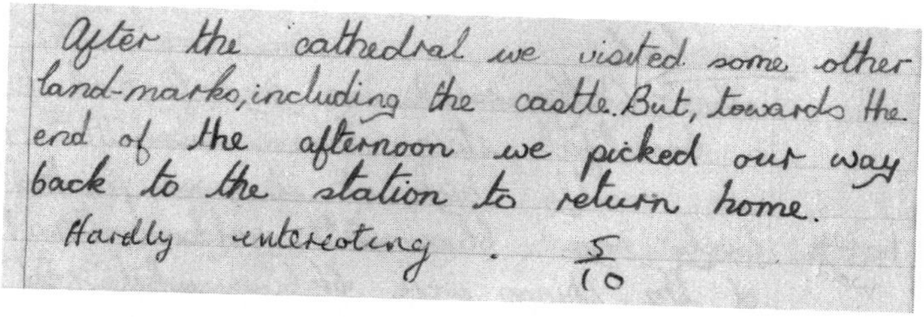
After the cathedral we visited some other land-marks, including the castle. But, towards the end of the afternoon we picked our way back to the station to return home.
Hardly interesting. 5/10

The words '5/10. Hardly interesting' are completely accurate, and I probably knew it even when I was writing it. My description of Islam in 'The five pillars of faith' has the single word 'Confused' at the end. Once again, I can't argue with that, though the later comment 'I would appreciate a little more work from you—you do not seem to be straining yourself' is a bit unfair. Well. Okay. Accurate. In one school report I get a D for German and a terse 'Disappointing'; in Physical Training I get a B and the single word 'Tries', which says more than a column of cautiously nurturing criticism.

I didn't feel crushed by these comments because I understood that the teacher knew how much effort I was putting into the task. That changes when I get to my Maths books. I'd gone all right at maths in primary school and had started off doing well when I started secondary school but then I started to slip. I hit that age when your peers become more important than your parents and you bridle at the yolk of authority. The full *you* emerges in all its warty, thin-skinned glory. A comment from a teacher a year earlier might have been met with a resigned shrug ('What can I do? She's a teacher and I'm just a kid') but now that same comment is met with hot, impotent fury. The injustice that you find yourself on the wrong end of at school you wear like a brand for the rest of your life.

Which brings me to my maths teacher. Maybe I deserved it, but I found myself on the end of some particularly harsh verbal floggings. Did he do it to other kids? Probably, but that's not for me to remember. My memory is of him sitting at his desk marking our books before audibly gasping, barking 'MacLean!' at which point I'd stand and he'd ask me what on earth I thought I'd been doing in some piece of long division or whatever. There's a certain force or power that emerges from the eye—we've all felt it when someone is watching us—and when that power is magnified 35-fold in a classroom of other kids, their eyes boring into you, relishing the fact that your humiliation means their own is stayed for another day, it takes a massive act of will to just stand there, take it and not charge headlong out the door and across the quad and out through the school gates. On one occasion I was asked to repeat an answer I'd given and I said, 'Ten point eighty-four'. I can still remember the number! And Mr Teacher stood from his seat.

'Ten point *what?*'

'Eighty-four,' I stammered.

'Eighty-four? Nonsense! *Eight* four. Eight *four*.'

My maths book is filled with the usual problems to be solved, some pages with smeared ink—the perennial left-hander's problem with fountain pens. Each page has a few ticks, but more crosses. And where my answer was particularly far out ('The average weight of each member of the team is 13 kg') there's the word 'Nonsense!' in red pen pressed so hard it almost bursts through the page. What made these comments sting was that I was genuinely trying. I just wasn't getting it.

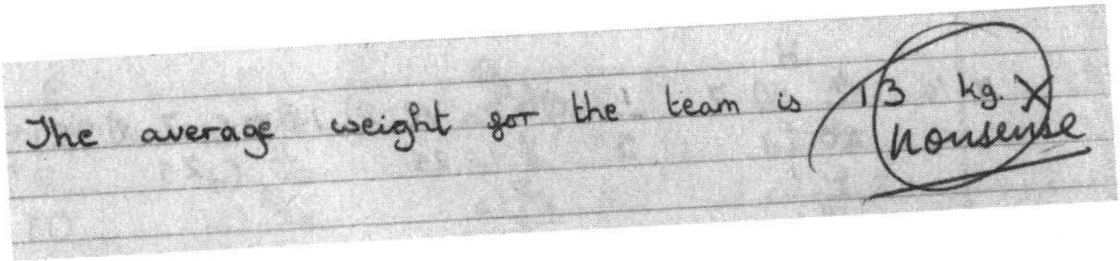

I'm in a reading group with a bunch of friends and each Christmas we have a bit of a get-together and a quiz and a dinner; it's all good fun. We mark our books out of ten. We know it's an imprecise art ('Could you really give that Alice Munro an eight when you only gave the Pat Barker a seven?!') but if nothing else it provides us with a benchmark against which we can flog some poor unsuspecting author. I record the books and our marks in an old purple exercise book and at one Christmas party I had the bright idea of adding up everyone's marks for the year: which was the 'best' book according to our system, and who was the harshest marker, who was the most generous. There were quite a few surprises and a couple of folk expressed amazement that they'd been so harsh or so generous. And then one of them had a look at my adding up.

Oh dear. I was back in the classroom, with the collective power of all those eyes boring down upon me.

MacLean? Stand up.

Nonsense!

* * *

In spite of my love of things that came in tins, I remember being pretty pleased that I managed to get this game of "Owzthat!" in the fancy new plastic tube.

I'm not sure if they still make "Owzthat!" or whether young lads would want to pass away a Science lesson by surreptitiously rolling the little hexagonal rods on their exercise books (to deaden the sound). There are two rods: one for the batting team and one for the bowling. The edges on the batting one are numbered 1, 2, 3, 4 and 6, while one edge has OWZTHAT. You roll and accrue runs until you roll OWZTHAT, at which point the bowler gets to roll his rod. This one has BOWLED, LBW, CAUGHT, NOT OUT and so on. It's not very sophisticated as entertainment goes.

There's a frail piece of paper inside with the rules to 'The cricket game for all weathers'. On its reverse there's a pencilled score that shows that I flogged Sid H with an unbeaten partnership between my ninth and tenth batsmen.

I had a little roll of the "Owzthat!", just for old times' sake. It was dead boring.

* * *

If I mention to The Wife that I once went on a school trip to Germany I usually get a twenty-minute broadside on how she never went anywhere outside New Lambton and anyway the nearest island was Indonesia which in 1975 was hardly a travel destination of choice for

Australian schools, unlike where *you* grew up with Europe right on your doorstep and so on and so forth.

It was amazing, really. I think I must have caught the first wave of my school's international focus, and this coincided with a time of prosperity on the home front. Mam was still at the shoe factory but Dad had got work on a big extension at the local paper mill so he was on a regular wage, he could eat at the staff canteen and—critically—each week he could buy a certain amount of paper products at cost price. Dad has always liked a bargain and bought everything he could up to his weekly limit: bog roll, kitchen rolls, tissues—both regular and 'man size'. Soon the back bedroom was stuffed with boxes to the point where it was like a TARDIS in reverse, much tinier on the inside than it looked from the outside.

But things were easier financially. We never talked about money around the house and I never knew if things were going well or not but I could sense it. Not long after the Three Day Week (Google it, kids) Dad had to go scouting all over the place for work and was in Yorkshire for a bit. But when the paper-mill work came along he was around, and not having to work odd hours. We'd always had shepherd's pie with baked beans on Thursday but around 1977 we started getting this piece of boot leather that was apparently steak. I'd have preferred shepherd's pie but we got steak, and I knew from this that times were good.

So we had a bit of money at the same time as the school started doing trips away, and I got to go to Germany. My main memories are of long hours on a bus, of singing endless dirty songs and of standing around looking at volcanic lakes. We came from the Lake District so bodies of water weren't all that much of an attraction to us but they were on the itinerary and so we were taken there to look at them. The best thing of all about Germany though was a legal drinking age of fourteen.

It was at this time that I started collecting beer mats. These were a standard collectible of the time and were produced in huge numbers so that schoolboys could pinch them when they sloped into pubs and conspired to get served. At the hotel we stayed in I made friends with a group of Germans who used to come to the hotel from the nearby town on a fleet of whining mopeds to drink das bier and play das card games. They taught me how to play Skat and I bought my own pack, thereby beginning a lifelong love of hanging around in boozers and gambling. If for nothing else, my school, I thank you for that.

I bought a ceramic stein as a symbol of my newly found manhood. It's probably the German equivalent of a stick of rock from Blackpool prom but I was rather pleased with it. I also have the little glass that we were given at Ernst Gattwinkel Weinbrau und Weinhandel when we went wine tasting (yes, wine tasting; don't all schools take their Year 9 students wine tasting?) but it was the beer that captured my imagination. The combination of legal alcohol and British schoolboys could, of course, have only one possible outcome. The last night before we took the long coach ride through to Belgium and the ferry terminal involved mass inebriation, vomit on the bathroom floor and lots of shouting from the teachers. (How dare we spend the last night getting drunk; that's their job!)

What did I learn from that educational journey, so dearly paid for by my hard-working parents? Belgian food is horrible. A volcanic lake is a volcanic lake, no matter where in the world it is. The water tastes different in Germany. Scooping up someone else's vomit from the bathroom floor with your fingers is deeply unpleasant. A British two-bob coin is almost exactly the same size as a German 50 pfennig coin, close enough to fool a jukebox into giving you five songs for the price of two. I'm not good at cards. I want to go back!

* * *

I lived in an almost entirely cashless economy until about the age of fourteen, when I got a Sunday paper round. It wasn't actually my round; these things were hard to come by and so the lad who got it subcontracted it out to me and another lad. It was 75p for four hours' work, which worked out at 37½p each, plus tips. I was giddy with my new wealth for a while and blew it on Top Trumps cards, little metal warrior figures, Subbuteo teams.

Once the idea of money had gotten its hooks into us we started to think more and more about it: how to get it, how to spend it. By the time we were turning sixteen we would come up with schemes, each one less feasible than the last. Until Pat hit the jackpot.

One of the lads in our group did weekend work for his dad, who owned and ran a small printery. He'd often do work for the school, and in my mind I can still see the cards he printed for fundraisers, school discos and so on: about 5 inches by 3 inches with a crenulated edge and a pink border, with funky black text in the middle. Whist drive! Celtic ceilidh!

Pat went into the printery with my friend and, one weekend, they printed off one thousand tickets to a Richie Blackmore's Rainbow concert in the town hall. At £2.50 a piece they fairly flew out the door, and by the end of the week Pat had gone to the Kawasaki dealer and bought himself a brand new 250 cc motorbike, cash, no questions asked.

It was great. We were in complete awe of him. Until his arrest, three or four days later. But I'm still in awe of him. What an amazing thing to even think of, let alone actually do. Pat: you are my hero.

* * *

I know all the arguments for not letting kids have too much screen time, and that our childhood involved lots of running

around in the fresh air and climbing trees and not coming home till dark. But I do envy the entertainment that modern kids have. I'm sure I would have loved all those games that involve hours and hours of wiggling your thumbs back and forth on a game console to chase monkeys around a temple or cut watermelons in half.

The Seventies was when children's TV in Britain became a force. Up until then it'd been seriously weak, lots of homemade puppets in black and white voiced by fusty Home Counties types. ('Shall we go into the garden? Clip clop! Clip clop!') It took programme makers years to drop the educational aspect of these shows, which meant that even a moderately good show could be spoiled by the didactic subtext that kids can smell a mile off.

I liked drawing and must have entered this competition. There were some TV shows that I watched not because they were any good; just because they were on telly. They were hosted by people like Bernard Cribbins and Michael Bentine, entertainers who'd been at the cutting edge in 1958 or 1963, but in 1974 they were up against Marc Bolan and that sexy presenter off *Magpie*. Bentine hosted a show called *Potty Time* which involved (guess what) puppets. It was so lame that I remember being both angry (at him) and embarrassed (for him) at the same time.

In spite of its glacially slow pacing and lack of dialogue I did enjoy *Vision On* with Tony Hart. This show must have cost about three shillings and sixpence to make; it was just Tony, some cardboard and a pen. Maybe some plasticine if the budget stretched that far. The educational aspect was in the creativity and the lack of speech, or hardly any at all. Tony did have a female offsider who did sign language for the limited talky bits. There was a section called The Gallery that showcased all the cack-handed drawings that Britain's kids had sent in, when they weren't playing "Owzthat!" or writing garbled letters to penfriends. I didn't ever send one in myself but I know for a fact that I did send one in to the John Menzies MONSTER painting competition and, to this day, I have yet to receive my Dr Who Monster Badge from Tom Baker.

* * *

When my own kids were at primary school in Australia they got introduced to The Game of Life. It was a role play affair, with the kids being assigned roles in an imaginary town: someone was the mayor, someone the fire chief, someone the policeman, someone a journalist, someone else the baker and so on.

I went to the presentation. The kids—nine and ten-year-olds—sat on the floor in a circle while the person selling it in (because of course this being school in the 21st century it turned out to be some kind of franchise deal) talked to them about their future, and how The Game of Life would make them adaptable and resilient and prepare them for what lay ahead. 'Statistics show that you will have five career changes in your lifetimes' said the presenter earnestly. The kids looked back in awe, most of them wondering what a career was. Then the presenter said, 'Some of the industries you will work in have yet to be invented' and 'The only constant in your future will be change'.

I've yet to see people working in many new industries now that didn't exist in 1978. The form might have shifted a bit but that's about it. (And anyway, if you're offering kids a brave new world with yet-to-be-imagined industries, why offer them roles like policeman, baker and journalist?) I find the message that 'the only constant is change' to be very troubling. It wasn't what most of those wide-eyed Year 5 and 6 kids needed to hear. Sure there'd be the odd Bill Gates type among them but for a fair chunk of those kids I know that school was about the only constant in their lives, and to be told by the grown-ups there that, basically, they had no idea what was going to happen next week was not the reassurance they needed.

Mixed in with my schoolbooks are a couple of mimeographed sheets of foolscap paper from my own school's careers advice day. There's a short instruction at the top of the first page followed by nine tables of twelve occupations. The idea is to list, from 1 to 12, the jobs in each table in order of desirability. 'Work quickly,' it says, 'as your first impressions are preferred.'

Exactly what my first impressions were of some of the jobs is difficult to tell; my numbering looks completely random. This is most likely because of the occupations on offer. In Table A, for instance, the jobs include (and these are absolutely true) 'scientist', 'bank manager', 'farmer' and 'concert pianist'. Even at the time I knew that 'scientist' was a fairly broad and unspecific term. And it sounded dead boring, nearly as boring as 'bank manager'. Farmers were just farmers. Half my friends' dads were farmers so it wasn't a career, as such, it was just being a farmer. My sister was in the school recorder ensemble, which had done very well at the Morecombe Eisteddfod, but I was also certain that that fact alone would not enhance my chances of becoming a concert pianist, no matter what my first impressions told me.

Table B is just as eclectic and random. It has 'radio announcer', 'industrial chemist', 'surgeon' and 'novelist'. Someone had to think this list up. To me a chemist was a place, not a person. It's where you went to get your holiday pictures developed or to try and shoplift a packet of johnnies. I would have guessed that a radio announcer was like a DJ, but maybe not exactly like a DJ. Surgeons and novelists were as common on the streets of my home town as unicorns and fallen stars.

Table C has 'playwright', 'meteorologist', 'fitter and turner'. Hooray! A job I'd heard of. I didn't exactly know what a fitter and turner did but I had friends whose dads did it. The fitting bit explained itself: they fitted things together. I wasn't sure about the turning part, but it probably had to do with lathes. Yeah, I could do that. Table D includes 'social worker', 'music critic', 'income tax assessor' and 'explorer'.

It was hard. You've been told not to think too hard about this, just zip through and tick the boxes. But when you see 'explorer' as an option you can't help but pause for a second. Is that possible? Are they telling me that I could really be an explorer? Or is it a secret test to see how far up yourself you are—you tick it and they come up afterwards, or maybe in front of the whole class, go 'Ah! And I believe we have a budding explorer in our midst!' (class sniggers, someone kicks someone else under the desk) 'Mister MacLean, apparently you believe that there are corners of the earth as yet to be tamed by the human hand.' All eyes on me. 'Where will your next expedition take you: The wilds of Preston, perhaps? The dark reaches of Milnethorpe?' Nah. Not ticking that.

But we've been told to work quickly and not think too hard about it. The careers adviser is a bloke with a Zapata moustache. None of us had seen him before; he was probably a casual teacher but we thought that maybe he was a special kind of teacher who went around deciding what jobs people would get, Cumbria County Council's early prototype of the Hogwarts sorting hat. We're working through our lists, not thinking too hard. Now he's looking at his watch, this teacher, and turning his fag packet round and round in his jacket pocket. On to Table E.

Table E has 'jewellery designer', 'bricklayer', 'dentist' and 'prospector'. Dad was a brickie and if I knew nothing else about my future I knew this one thing: it was that I'd never be a brickie. These days you can earn a motza laying bricks but back in the day it was, to use my Dad's own words, shit-house. There was no job security, and whole gangs would get laid off at the drop of a hat. The days were long and hard and I remember on days when there was a heavy frost the bricks were frozen together. He was clear about this: you'll never be a brickie. But a prospector? Hmm. Table F has 'botanist', 'optician', 'GPO technician' and 'organist'. I thought (OK, still think) that GPO technician might have been either a postman or someone who works at the sorting office. I'd seen two organists in my life: the bloke at the bottom of Blackpool Tower, and Winnie Dawson at the church. But if I'd been looking to pick up on the fourth occupation in each category as the 'out there' one (explorer, prospector) then maybe organists led carefree, almost dangerous, lives.

Table G has 'astronomer', 'youth club worker', 'record librarian (music)', 'plasterer'. That blew off the theory of the fourth occupation as being wild and crazy; our Uncle George was a plasterer and his life was neither carefree nor dangerous. Table H has 'physiotherapist', 'postal clerk', 'window dresser' and 'dance band leader'. Rounding up the list is Table I with 'market gardener', 'welder', 'textile designer', 'poet'.

It was all too much. What was the difference between a GPO technician and a postal clerk? Did one sort the letters and the other deliver them? If so, why didn't they just say 'postman'? Why would they offer me 'window dresser' and 'textile designer'? Had they accidentally given me the girls' list? Poet or dance band leader? Was that like the explorer and prospector all over again? 'One of our group considers himself to be a future Shelley or Yeats!' (class sniggers) 'Please do stand up, Mister MacLean, and entertain us with one of your odes!' As for dance band leader, well, really, now you're just taking the piss.

At the time I thought that this list was just thrown together during morning tea by a teacher. It seemed too nutty and random. Now I can see something else going on. These teachers knew where we were headed. For girls there was the possibility of some secretarial work, or maybe nursing or, for the select few, teaching. For the lads it was the gas board, the army and the shipyard, with those with half a brain or a skerrick of ambition heading to sixth form college and a polytechnic or even university. They knew this, and now I respect them for throwing in impossible 'occupations' like 'prospector', 'explorer', 'poet' and 'dance band leader'. Why not?

I filled the boxes in, from 1 to 12, and then the scores were aggregated through some complex set of algorithms, and out popped the three suggested occupations that were ideal to my personality type: forester, gamekeeper, artist.

Without further ado I completely ignored this list. Instead, I did what Mam and Dad told me to do: I put my application in to the shipyard and became an electrician.

N.L.P.L. 1983-84
DIV. 2. 3RD PLACE
LONDON TAVERN
M. McLEAN

Box 3

For a long, long time I hankered after the university education I never had. To be specific, it wasn't so much the education that I was interested in but I ached to live in 'digs' where everyone wore paint-spattered dungarees and went to life drawing classes and parties and drank wine. And, most important of all, had all that sex with posh Home Counties totty.

Luckily for me, the world, and the posh girls of the Home Counties, I didn't do all that. I would have been the worst kind of student, the dour Northerner with a massive chip on his shoulder that everyone avoids in the common room. Instead I was privileged to get an apprenticeship in one of the great trades during the final days of British industry.

The first few months were just like school. We got issued with overalls and a toolkit (which we very pleased with until we realised that the cost of this toolkit would be deducted from our wages) and we signed the *Official Secrets Act* because the yard we worked in made ships and submarines for the Royal Navy. We got shown old films on the kinds of horrible injuries that result when young men horse around with a length of angle bar and a high-speed grinding wheel. We learnt about the Great Divide that existed between the black trades (the platers, welders, caulkers and shipwrights) and the outfitters (the electricians, carpenters, pipe workers and painters).

We sparks were divided into two groups. One group was instructed by a laid-back guy nearing retirement who did a bit of refereeing for local football and was generally considered to be all right. The other group, my group, was instructed by a Territorial Army sergeant who had a box-shaped build and a skull that pushed out from his shoulders without the need for a neck. He was known as Slabhead.

We raced our screaming mopeds to work and we got paid and we did man things with metal and cables but then, after work, it was like we were school kids again and we had to go off to learn about the thinking side of being an electrician at the local technical college. It was man things from half seven till half four then back to being a kid from half five at night. We did block release for one week in every three or four, plus a few nights of evening class. This was not on because, in our minds, we were now men and we'd cast off childish things, like sitting at a desk and being talked at by some hollow-eyed loser in a corduroy jacket. Lads would openly slump forward on their desks and sleep during classes, which was the late Seventies equivalent to scrolling through Facebook on your iPhone.

The worst part was the hour between finishing work at 4.30 pm and starting evening class at 5.30. An hour wasn't long enough even for the bristling power machine that was my Honda SS50 to make the 14-mile round trip to home and back and so I found myself for endless winter nights hanging around town with a tray of chips and gravy, standing in the doorways of closed shops trying to avoid the rain, watching people go home.

In the trade school, Slabhead taught us the basics of electricity. He used a lot of mnemonics which I thought at the time were stupid but have proven themselves by staying with me for over thirty years. Want to remember what the colours of a three-cord flex are? Over to you, Slabhead: 'Green's the earth cable, right? Green, like grass. That's on the Earth. Right? Blue. Blue's the neutral cable. The sky's blue, like something that's neutral. It's not anything: it's just sky. Right? Brown. Brown's the live wire. Touch that an' you'll shit yer pants. Right?' Right.

We learnt how to benchsmith flat bar to make cable runs, how to make cable clips out of copper strips, how to correctly offer the screwdriver blade to the head of a number 8 half-inch black japanned screw, how to strip down an alternator and replace the carbon brushes, and dozens of other tasks that were, in the main, entirely irrelevant to what we'd be doing over the next few years. That's because we were shipyard electricians and we'd spend most of our apprenticeship threading huge, fat cables through submarine bulkheads or banding them into position with strips cut from thick coils of galvanised metal tape.

But at the time it was still kind of exciting. The first time you wire up a battery to a lamp using three switches and you run all the tests on it and then you switch it on and it works . . . well, there are few things in my adult life that have matched that thrill and sense of achievement. Exciting as it all was, though, it was really a prelude to the Real Thing: the moment when we left trade school after nine months and went into the shipyard proper. This is when we really became men.

* * *

This is my first toolbox, with my first clocking on number stencilled on the end: 301.

There must have been a reason why these two massive spanners—an open-ended and ring spanner, 24 mm at one end and 27 mm at the other—were included in the toolkit but I have yet to fathom what that reason was. I've carried them to dozens of building sites and shipyards in Britain and Australia but have never ever used them.

We also got a set of BA spanners, which I keep in one of Dad's Golden Virginia baccie tins. Some of these I have used, once or twice, over the course of my working life, but never in a shipyard.

They all have my name engraved on them, as we were instructed to do when we first got the toolkit. I remember at the time wondering what the hell kind of work we'd be doing as electricians that needed gigantic ring spanners and teeny-tiny Action Man spanners. If anyone ever found out, please drop me a line.

* * *

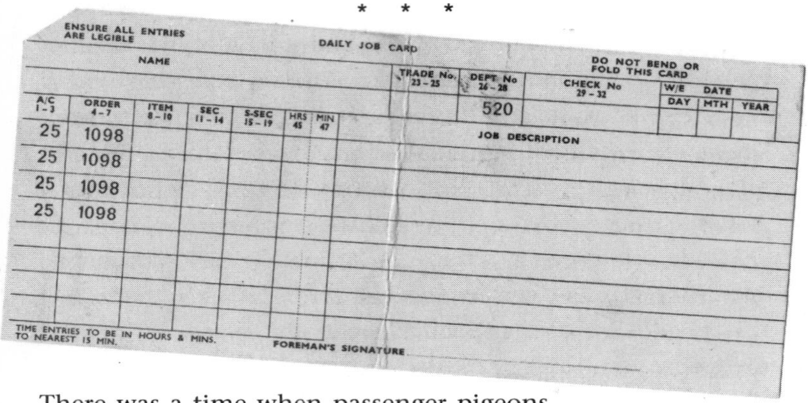
ENSURE ALL ENTRIES ARE LEGIBLE

DAILY JOB CARD

NAME

DO NOT BEND OR FOLD THIS CARD

TRADE No. 23 – 25 | DEPT No 26 – 28: 520 | CHECK No 29 – 32 | W/E DATE: DAY | MTH | YEAR

A/C 1 – 3	ORDER 4 – 7	ITEM 8 – 10	SEC 11 – 14	S-SEC 15 – 19	HRS 45	MIN 47	JOB DESCRIPTION
25	1098						
25	1098						
25	1098						
25	1098						

TIME ENTRIES TO BE IN HOURS & MINS. TO NEAREST 15 MIN.

FOREMAN'S SIGNATURE

There was a time when passenger pigeons flew across the skies of North America in flocks so dense that the sun was blotted out for minutes at a time. People pointed their guns at the heavens and pulled the triggers for the simple joy of watching two dozen birds tumble earthwards for every cartridge spent. And then, one day, there was only one single passenger pigeon left: Martha, who was kept in a cage at Cincinnati Zoo. And when Martha died there were no more passenger pigeons.

There was a time in my life when time cards were like passenger pigeons, and if I'd told my 1978 self that one day they'd be gone I'd have been struck dumb at the very thought. How this one, this Martha of the time card world, ended up at home is a mystery. Maybe it was a bookmark for *The Miracle of the Rose* or *The Go-between* or *Metamorphosis* or whatever Penguin Modern Classic it was that I was grinding my way through at the time.

As apprentices we had to fill in books each Friday morning with details of what we'd been doing that week, and a few notes on what we'd learnt, and every few weeks someone was supposed to look at these books and maybe test us on ship's terms like 'deckhead' and 'coaming' and 'derrick'.

The problem for an apprentice is that you're the flattened base of a very broad pyramid. You don't get to see the interesting stuff happening at the pinnacle, you just do the crap. Which is fair enough: if I wanted a radar wired up on an aircraft carrier I wouldn't have got me to do it. I was a feckless dreamer more interested in punk rock records and beer and motorbikes and girls. And so, far from being taught the intricacies of wiring up junction boxes or heat-proofing a fire alarm system we did the drone work: feeding endless miles of electrical cables around submarines and ships.

They're not like houses, where you can hide the cables in the roof space or wall cavity. During its construction every compartment (that's a room, in ship talk) is filled with miles and miles of coiled-up cables: big fat ones like black salamis and skinny ones like liquorice straps. To get them into the next compartment they have to be fed through a waterproof gland in the bulkhead (wall) or deckhead (ceiling), then strapped to metal frames. Then they're coiled up again in the next compartment and the process is repeated over and over until your cable has reached its destination. Until you've done this for a year or two you've no idea how many miles and miles of cables there are in a sub, and that's all most of us did for months on end.

And so every week we were challenged to find something inventive to say about how we had coiled up a cable, fed one end through a hole, pulled it through from the other side and then coiled it up again.

I think that if I closed my eyes and held a pen in my hand I could accurately fill this time card in based on muscle memory alone.

* * *

A huge amount of energy was invested by the workers of the shipyard into the process of not working. People would spend days and weeks fine-tuning schemes that gave the impression of industry whilst achieving absolutely nothing. I learnt early on in my career the technique required to put a piece of metal into a vice then move a file back and forth across the metal in such a way that it *sounded* like you were filing the metal and *looked* like you were filing the metal but without removing so much as a millimetre from its surface.

Much of the energy conserved by not working was invested in the creation of top quality brew boxes. These were usually ex-NATO packing cases, modified to become your own little world, the place where you stored your mug, your teabags, your paper and your cock books, your back-up Pot Noodles and—if there was room—a few tools. The best brew boxes had a slab of foam gaffer-taped to the lid to make them into a portable stool. Some of the more permanent ones had been modified to the point where they looked like the throne of some African king: pure works of art.

At brew time we'd come off the boat and head into the workshop. Once again, this required careful timing to maximise the amount of time away from the workplace but without making it so obvious that you'd either turn up too early and get sprung by a foreman or leave the boat too early and get caught in your absence by the sudden arrival of the foreman at your workplace.

I loved brew time. First thing in the morning, around twenty past seven, most people were still too tired or hungover to do much other than mutter a bit, grab their tools, get a bit of gear from the store and head towards the boat. The foremen came out of their glass-walled office and shooed everyone out. Here comes Billy Gingham with his rib-tickling catch-cries: 'Hands off cocks: on with socks', 'Break it up, it's not a fuckin union meeting', 'Don't have your soup in a group'. Did he lie in bed at night thinking them up? Totter Charlton with his folding ruler that he clacked like a crocodile's jaws. Donnie O'Shay, with his breath that reeked of barley wine. And off we'd move, a slow, bovine herd, to pretend to work for an hour and a half, till nine o'clock brew time.

That's when everyone perked up. There'd be a bit of high jinks around the steaming water urn. After you'd fished your tea bag out of your mug you could, if you were careful, place it on someone's shoulder without their noticing and slope off. It'd take a second or two before the scalding hot water soaked through their overalls, at which point they'd leap 10 feet into the air and break into a hilarious highland dance, while you sniggered from the safety of your brew box. How we laughed!

People would get their papers out. It was mostly the red tops: the *Sun*, the *Mirror*, the *Star*, the occasional *Mail*. Maybe even an *Express*. Some of these papers had pictures of ladies with no tops on. I read that when the *Sun* introduced Page 3 the sub-eds would show the pictures to the female journalists to get their endorsement; they didn't want anything too smutty. Apparently the girls' smile was always considered to be their most important asset. Personally, I do not remember a single one of these girls' smiles. They were known collectively, these topless ladies, as 'the tits', as in 'What are the tits like today?' *The Star* printed their half-naked ladies in colour on a Monday, and so these lasses were known as 'the colour tits'. In the blacksmith shop at one of the docks they had all the colour tits on the wall, every one of them since the first one.

Page 3 is a social phenomenon that's become part of the fabric of modern Britain, though at the time it was new enough to be remarkable. There have been theses written on Page 3 and arguments and counter-arguments of it as an expression of the new feminism or neo-conservatism. But for all the gazillion words on the subject, to the men who looked at those pictures they were just 'the tits'.

* * *

My first motorised vehicle was a two-stroke KTM scrambler missing its gearshift. A new gearshift cost the insane sum of 11 pounds and so I got by with a pair of mole grips clamped to the spindle, leaning down to make gear changes by hand. What could possibly go wrong?

The next was a 49 cc Honda, a four-stroke with about 0.01 horsepower of deep, torquey grunt. This was the monster that took me to work and back until I turned seventeen and my licence allowed me to upgrade to something more powerful, in this case a 175 cc BSA Bantam. All these bikes were old when I got them and had been flogged to within an inch of their lives by previous owners, so night after night was spent bolting back together all the broken or fallen-off bits that had come away on the ride to work or back. I knew I wasn't king of the road—the really desirable moped was the Yamaha FS1E, the Fizzer—but being independently mobile was a wonderful thing.

The down side was that getting anywhere was a bloody nightmare. If there was a band on in Liverpool or Manchester (no one ever came to Cumbria) then it was a two or three hour trip south, then another hour roving around trying to find the venue. Google Maps? What's that? So I should hardly have been surprised when, two weeks into my apprenticeship, my parents wouldn't let me go to Manchester on a Tuesday night to see Devo. Just because I'd started a new job and just because it was a Tuesday night and just because it'd take me six hours there and back on a Honda moped that was deeply unreliable and just because I didn't actually know where the venue was but I'd seen it advertised in the *New Musical Express* and . . .

Oh, how I railed! I was, after all, sixteen years old and therefore a complete man and the owner of two pairs of overalls and a toolkit and therefore in charge of my own destiny, though our Mam seemed to think otherwise.

I was thinking about those wild desperate times when places like Leeds and Carlisle and Preston were faraway centres that, from coastal Cumbria, seemed as distant as glimmering galaxies captured by the Hubble telescope. Modern travel is ridiculously easy. People fly to Barcelona from Manchester to watch midweek football matches. A wee while back a few of us went down to Sydney from Newcastle to see the Buzzcocks. We set off mid afternoon, had playlists going on the car stereo, stopped at Gordon for a Thai meal and, after we were guided by sat-nav to the venue's parking area, I swaggered up to the ticket office, handed over my shiny credit card and picked up the tickets that I'd booked online weeks earlier.

Do I want those olden days back? No.

Do I wish I'd sneaked off and seen Devo anyway? Of course. Every single day.

* * *

The shipyard wasn't a single place, it was a whole series of places that covered a vast area. There were gun workshops and places with endless rows of lathes and massive sheds where the hulls of submarines slowly rotated on gigantic tumbrels as their sections were welded, caulked, ground back and re-welded to ensure a joint that could withstand the immense pressures of the deep oceans. There were the docks too, where boats were fitted out once launched, and each dock had its own village of trades to turn these metal shells into proud ships.

To get into each workshop and dock you had to go through a security gate, past the greasy-moustached army part-timers who passed as security guards. And outside each gate there was a brew wagon.

A brew wagon is a wee mobile van that stocks your necessaries for life inside the yard, for once inside it was a bugger of a job to get out if you'd forgotten to buy milk or a paper. They stocked the *Mirror*, the *Sun*, the *Star*, the *Mail*. They stocked tea bags and milk and Pot Noodles and Yorkie bars and crisps. They stocked every cock book you could imagine and some you couldn't. (Some were 'Swedish'. It was the 1970s and in the fevered imagination of a teenage Northerner, the mere word 'Swedish' conjured up the kinds of erotic fantasies that still cause the backs of my knees to break out in a sweat.) They stocked Benson & Hedges and Silk Cut and No. 6 and Capstan and Golden Virginia and pipe tobacco in round tins with funny olden times names and floral smells. They stocked Old Jamaica and Turkish Delight and Curly Wurlies and cigarette lighters and Wrigley's spearmint gum. They stocked everything.

You didn't want to arrive too late for work if you needed to get to the brew wagon before you went in and clocked on. When you pushed your clocking-on card into the big clock there'd be an almighty thump like God had pressed a key on a gigantic typewriter, and your card was stamped with a black 7.28 or 7.25 or whatever time it was. But after 7.30 the ribbon changed to red and, from 7.31 onwards, you'd get that horrible sinking feeling of knowing your wages would be docked a quarter of an hour for being late. Three red stamps in a week and it was off to the glass-walled foreman's office for a bollocking.

The low moan of the first hooter went at 7.25. If you were in the queue at the brew wagon at 7.25 you could work out if you had time to get your paper and your Pot Noodle and your fags and your milk then leg it down to the clocking-on station and stay in the black. They had a pretty smooth system and could fire out an order in a matter of seconds and have you on your way quick smart, then the brew man could get ready for the next wave of arrivals at eight o'clock. This was the 'staff': the people who worked in the drawing offices and management and admin. We started at half seven and 'staff' started after eight. They had their own toilets and all kinds of things did 'staff', and a bit of a different menu at the canteen, or so I'd heard.

It's this one day and the clocks had just chugged over to 7.25 and everyone in the queue knows this because the first hooter starts its big long gurn that floats over the shipyard and the town and even, if the wind was right, to my house a few miles up the coast where our Mam would be getting ready for a day in the shoe factory. The queue skips along: 'A *Mirror* and a pinta milk an twenty Benson'; 'A *Sun* and a packeta Chewits; 'a *Mail* and a *Readers' Wives* and a Mars bar'. Then it gets to me and I say, 'I'll have a chicken Pot Noodle and a Caramac and a *Guardian.*'

Everything stops. The brew man stops. The queue stops. I think the hooter stopped. I'd asked for a Big Paper.

When I did the Sunday paper round there was a family on the new estate, the one that folk called Toy Town, who got the *Observer* and that was one of the first Big Papers I ever read, and also one of the first to have a colour supplement. If I got a wiggle on I could find a bit of time to pull that colour supplement out and look at it before I got to Toy Town and delivered it. The *Observer* colour supplement was magic, it was exotic and cosmopolitan. Those interviews with people like Doctor Kissinger or one of the Dimblebys and those photographic essays of wars in the Horn of Africa or footballers and their Jensen Interceptors. The Big Papers were like the wardrobe to Narnia; somehow, by reading them, I could step into the world of Marvellous Things and Beautiful People. Most days I got the *Mirror*; I liked Keith Waterhouse and Paul Foot and Andy Capp and it was a proper Left-wing paper. But now I wanted a Big Paper.

The brew man narrows his eyes at me and says, 'I'll have to see how I'm fixed.' I knew what this meant: the gurny git had plenty of *Guardians* under the counter, waiting to be brought out for 'staff' when they sauntered in, but he was buggered if he was going to start selling Big Papers to the 7.30 hoi polloi.

'Hurry the fuck up!' shouts someone a bit behind me.

Brew man knows if he gives me a Big Paper now I'll be back, wanting one tomorrow, and that that means some ponce on 'staff' will ask for a *Guardian* and he'll have to simper 'Oh, I'm terribly sorry, but I appear to have sold out'. He could have just ordered more and made a greater profit but this was 1980 and we still hadn't got to grips with Mrs Thatcher and the free market economy. So he looks at me and pretends to scout around under his counter and then someone else shouts 'Fuckin hurry up!' and so, with a face like the proverbial bull-dog licking piss off a thistle, he pulls one out and hands it over.

It wasn't, of course, the first Big Paper into the work-shop—Big Peter got the *Daily Telegraph*—but it was the first one that I'd bought, and among the first that my group of mates had seen. We crowded round it at brew time. We were surprised to see that it had a sports section, and even had the racing fixtures in it, just like a real paper. I don't know what we expected—maybe page after page of densely typed politics with no pictures. It had a TV guide and even cartoons: one was called Doonesbury, which was political in some way I didn't understand, and another by Steve Bell, which was also political. Neither of them were funny as far as I could see. I wondered: is that how it is in the big papers? Even the cartoons aren't funny?

But I thought it was great. I was converted, and from that day on the brew man reluctantly kept a *Guardian* aside for me. I felt different, but I wasn't different. If someone held up the *Sun* or the *Star* and said, 'Check out these tits!' I sure enough would do. Turns out that some habits are harder to break than others.

* * *

Trophies: they're rubbish. We've got a box in the back shed with The Wife's old squash trophies and my soccer and football trophies. They're all, to a one of them, ugly looking things made out of cheap, nasty materials. Not one of them has my name spelt on it as it appears on my birth certificate; 'MacLean' is only seven letters but it's amazing how many ways it can be gotten wrong.

This trophy is different. I love it, and it's probably the only one I'd keep. It's made of the highest quality sterling silver—I know this because it's turned a cacky grey–brown colour, and only the highest quality sterling silver tarnishes like that—and it's mounted on a teak-style base that, at a glance, could be mistaken for moulded plastic. The plate upon the base says:

N.L.P.L. 1983-84
Div. 2. 3rd. place
London Tavern
M. McLean

The NLPL was the North Lonsdale Pool League and this was from the Wednesday night comp. There were endless rounds of leagues going on and on any given night there'd be ladies' darts or men's pool, car-loads of folk from other pubs arriving to take your pub on or you and a load of other folk piling into cars to take their pub on, and big trays of sandwiches going round at the end of the night, and then a lock-in.

I don't remember taking the pool comp very seriously, which is lucky because this trophy is what my kids would once have described as an 'epic fail'. First place? No. Second? No. Division 1? Um . . . nope. It's like an early prototype of the 'I participated' certificate handed out in primary schools. I love it.

* * *

After the Honda moped I upgraded to a series of BSA Bantams. I passed my test on a Bantam. It didn't have indicators and so I had to do all those olden times hand signals that made me look like a policeman out of a wartime movie. By passing my test the world of unlimited capacity motorcycles was opened up to me. After being sent over the bonnet of a car and getting the insurance money for one BSA I went for a Triumph Tiger. I can still see the look on our Mam's face when I pulled into the driveway on that. Then, in about 1981, I bought a brand new 650 cc Thunderbird from the recently re-opened Meriden factory, which had gone broke a few years earlier but was now operating as a cooperative. It was the most money I'd ever spent on anything, and remains the only new vehicle I've ever bought.

Six-fifty doesn't seem like much of a capacity now—I have a friend who's Ducati is 1300 cc—but back then it was as much as some cars. Okay, so those cars were Hillman Imps but they were still cars. The 81 Thunderbird was a stroke-shortened version of the 750 Bonneville, which was itself a bored out version of the 650. The result was a boxy, revvy engine that didn't have a brilliant top speed—maybe one-ten with a steep incline and a tailwind—but was responsive and could get you into and out of as much trouble as you liked. Apparently, I liked lots.

In the County of Cumbria, Petty Sessional Division of Barrow-in-Furness, information has this day been laid before me, the undersigned, by Hugh Maxwell Ball, Chief Superintendent of Police, Divisional Headquarters, that you, Mark Douglas MacLean, at Barrow-in-Furness, in the County first aforesaid, did drive a motor bicycle on a certain restricted road called Abbey Road, at a speed exceeding 40 miles per hour, contrary to Section 74 of the Road Traffic Regulation Act, 1967 and Section 203 of the Road Traffic Act, 1972. You are therefore summoned to appear before the Magistrates' Court at Duke Street, Barrow-in-Furness . . .

Statement of Facts

At 7.20 a.m. on Monday, 21st May, the defendant rode a motor cycle along Abbey Road, Barrow-in-Furness. The speed of this vehicle was checked by means of speedometer and was found to be 62 miles per hour reducing to 55 miles per hour. Abbey Road at this point was restricted to a speed limit of 40 miles per hour. The defendant was stopped, cautioned and told the facts would be reported.

Statement of Facts

At 7.25 a.m. on Tuesday, 3rd April, the defendant rode a motor cycle along Walney Road, Barrow-in-Furness. The speed of this vehicle was checked by means of speedometer and was found to be 45 miles per hour. Walney Road at this point was restricted to a speed limit of 30 miles per hour. The defendant was stopped, cautioned and told the facts would be reported.

Statement of Facts

At 7.10 a.m. on Friday, 9th October, the defendant rode a motor cycle . . .

You get the drift.

That bike offered me more freedom than I'd ever had. The other bikes were okay but were old and a bit knackered. They were also made in England, which should have set alarm bells ringing in my head but I developed a mindless loyalty to British bikes that I still have to this day. The other bikes were like cranky relatives that you had to pay constant attention to otherwise they'd sulk and not work for you. I spent endless freezing winter hours on the concrete floor of our garage doing things to those bikes, an endless routine of maintenance just to make them fit to get me to work and home again the next day. The Thunderbird just went.

And the speed was intoxicating. I had a phase of riding with my eyes closed to see how far I'd get before I chickened out and opened them. This was up around the winding roads of the Lake District, not in traffic of course. I wasn't stupid! When you're young and a nobody in the world there's a great deal of pleasure to be had in haring around as part of a big motorcycle pack. I don't think we ever did anything bad, and we couldn't get served in any pubs ('No helmets No leathers') so we just cruised around, burning up fossil fuels and pulling up at roadside vans to eat bacon sarnies and drink sweet tea.

When I got more adventurous I headed towards mainland Europe. The shipyard closed down for the last week of July and first week in August; it was called Shipyard Fortnight and pretty well every business in the area shut down with it because just about every other business either depended on the shipyard or employed the spouses of those working in the yard. Me and my mates annoyed the French for a season or two but then decided that we'd like to annoy other members of the Common Market. I went to a travel agent in town to get some information on camp sites and things in Germany, Italy and Spain and the travel agent gave me the addresses of each country's tourism agency. I wrote off and, while the ones for Italy and Spain were what I'd expected, the one for Germany was not. I'd been given the address for the Deutsche Demokratische Republik—East Germany, in the old money—and this was a perfect revelation. You can actually go to East Germany?

I got all excited, went into the travel agents and got the addresses for the tourism agencies for other Eastern Bloc countries—Poland, Hungary, Yugoslavia and Romania—and back came these amazing packages full of maps and cultural information, often in German but sometimes in English. I took them in to work but not many of the lads were very keen; we were, after all, working on nuclear submarines for the Royal Navy at the height of the Cold War and though people's concerns might seem silly from the distance of thirty-plus years there was a general sense of suspicion about that part of the world. On the news there'd be occasional stories about British 'plane enthusiasts' who had 'accidentally wandered' across some unmarked border to photograph aeroplanes in Bulgaria and ended up locked away in a filthy communist prison. We'd all signed the *Official Secrets Act* on our first day at work and it didn't seem too far removed to think that travelling to the home of the Stasi might attract the wrong kind of attention.

We ended up with a compromise: across the top of Italy, down through Yugoslavia and into Greece. Tito's Yugoslavia was seen as more open than other Soviet-controlled countries; indeed, there were people we knew who had been on holiday to the Aegean Coast. So off we set, a bunch of naive Northerners on the lookout for good times. I had six days' leave accrued and so I tacked this onto my Shipyard Fortnight which gave me three and a bit weeks, with the intention of 'falling ill' in the last week. There'd be a bollocking when I got back but it would give me a whole month off. Unimaginable.

We annoyed the French and the Italians and for a little bit the Yugoslavs, then got a ferry from Ljubljana to Corfu. This was another revelation to me. I met people who were not on holiday for a fortnight, or three weeks, or even a month. They seemed to be on leave forever. I met a couple of Australians and they asked me about where I came from. I told them and it turned out they'd visited there, or nearby, and knew the area quite well. I asked them where they were from and they said, 'Tennant Creek', which of course resulted in a blank stare from me and laughter from them. They drew a map of Australia in the dirt and asked me to point to where I thought Tennant Creek might be: more laughter. Can you point to where Sydney is? I gamely pointed to somewhere near Brisbane.

They told me about Tennant Creek, where they were teachers. It sounded wild, amazing. And they told me that they were on twelve months' long-service leave. This 'long-service leave' was something that I had to have explained to me. I'd used every ounce of guile to stretch my holiday to just over three weeks, and here they were being paid for a year. To go on holiday. It seemed amazing, beyond comprehension. And this place, this Tennant Creek, sounded incredible too. I looked at the map of Australia in the dirt and began to hatch a plan.

* * *

From the perspective of the Australian Government's migration bureaucracy, Britain is divided into South and North. If you have to go in for an interview for a visa or residency status and you live in the South you go to Australia House in London and if you're in the North you go to Edinburgh. Some years after that night in a campground in Corfu I found myself in Edinburgh, along with lots of other Scots and English Northerners, waiting for such an interview. The weather was bracing in the way that folk in Auld Reekie might describe as 'fine'; that is, there was no Force 9 gale driving sleet into your face at a 45-degree angle. Inside Australia House it was nice and warm and there was a TV showing documentaries in the cheerful Ken Done colours of the period. This was before the renewed wave of pride and assertiveness that followed the Bicentennial celebrations and so the films were more of the Skippy and Rolf Harris variety, a shy pride veiled by an eye-rolling self-deprecating humour: Check us out! Weird, huh?

As well as the people preparing for their interviews there was a crowd of your common or garden punters who I'm sure had just come in off the street for a few minutes to get the feeling back into their extremities. I wondered at the time how many people had simply come in to get warm ended up plucking a leaflet from the carousel, filling it in and then accidentally found themselves in Australia. I actually know one person who did just that because I met him in Alice Springs. Like me, Patrick was an electrician and was taking his trade test after recently arriving in the Territory. It'd been pissing down rain one day and he'd just gone into Australia House for a quick warm-up and then, somehow, almost without him realising it, nine months later he was on a plane to the promised land.

The weather is a common theme of difference between Britain and Australia. Britain is grey, dark, wet. My kids, Australian born, claim that it doesn't know how to rain properly in Britain; the sky just leaks all the time like a tap with a busted washer. Australia meanwhile has tropical cyclones, catastrophic bushfires and rains that almost wash state capital cities into the ocean. It got so hot last summer that the Bureau of Meteorology had to add a new colour, purple, to its heat chart. That sums it up: not that there needed to be a new colour, but that the colour was purple. There is no weather condition in Britain that would ever by signified by the colour purple—they'd just dig another darker shade of grey out of a cupboard at the Met Office.

The winter weather forecast of my teenage years revolved around cloud cover. If there were clouds it would be raining, sleeting or snowing. I had boots and overtrousers and waxed-cotton gloves and so I knew that on my motorbike I'd get cold and wet but at least I'd remain upright. If there were no clouds then there'd be a frost. It'd be cold, I wouldn't get wet, but there would be ice. Lots of ice. The worst was a few days of rain and snow followed by a few days of clear skies and hard frosts.

I never enjoyed ice riding (go figure), and while it did teach me an awful lot about reading the road it always felt like trial by ordeal.

One day I was winding my way down the hill to Bottom Flats when the Triumph Thunderbird that was underneath me and was going forwards was now no longer underneath me and we're both sliding sideways into the hedge. Though I've been stuck under the backs of pick-up trucks and thrown over the bonnets of sedans this was not a 'crash' but a depressingly common winter's morning experience. I don't know how often over the years I laid down a Honda or a KTM or a Bantam or a Tiger or whatever bike it was that I was trashing at that particular moment.

The difference this time was I'd laid down the Tbird. While the Meriden cooperative had staggered back into half-life long enough to bang out some moderately decent bikes there were still some seriously old-school flaws in the production process. There were lots of things about my brand-new Tbird that would have been laughed out of a Honda showroom ten years earlier: the place where a rev counter should be was replaced by an oil light set-up that looked as though it had been made out of an old toilet roll on *Blue Peter*; the indicators were bought, sight unseen, from a guy in Germany who had a stack of them in his lock-up; and, though the rear foot pegs folded (as had all foot pegs on all motorcycles since about 1974) the front foot pegs were made to the same specs as those for the 1948 Speed Twin. They were made out of a single, bolted-on piece of pig iron, the kind of thing that Henry VIII's shipwrights used to fasten down the planks on the *Mary Rose*. So when I laid the bike down the peg (a) gouged out a deep trough in the bitumen and (b) eventually bent out of shape in a way that would have torn my calf muscle off if I'd been unlucky. I limped in to work and unbolted it at brew time and took it down, with the straight one off the opposite side, to the blacksmiths forge.

The forge was unworldly, like a set from an early Peter Jackson film: dark and grimy and hot on the coldest day. It also had that famously complete collection of colour Star Birds on display.

When I came in men were lounging around on brew boxes and showed little interest, at least until they realised what the job was. Then the tone changed. This was a foreigner, and as such it received the kind of treatment reserved for only this kind of job. Men that could barely show any interest in their paid work immediately sprang to life. They took the bent peg from me, and its straight sibling, and told me to come back in the afternoon.

When I came back the peg was absolutely perfect. When the same thing happened a few weeks later and I skidded down the road again, I took the peg back down the forge. This time I didn't have to wait long or bring the straight peg for comparison as, when they straightened the peg the first time, they'd made a jig for future reference. So much care and forethought and attention to detail. If only half of that had gone in to the building of submarines!

* * *

I had no political tuition; we were a household that got both the Right-wing newspaper the *Sun* and Left-wing *Mirror*, but we never talked politics. The exception perhaps was the lead-up to the 1979 election when our Mam decided it was about time they kicked those useless buggers out and handed the country over to a woman. I don't know how many Tory policies Mam could have listed but Margaret Thatcher's addled metaphor of running the country along the lines of a household budget became a strong narrative of the period, and persists to this day.

Here are two of my diary entries, in full, from that fateful year:

Thursday, 3 May 1979. Slabhead gave me his mother's kettle to fix. Terrible afternoon, I cocked it up and now it's even more broken and won't turn on or off. Went to Earthquake at dinnertime and bought new Angelic Upstarts single. Thumbed it home after night school. Watched an Errol Flynn film and then This is Your Life, *but went to bed halfway through. Maggie got in for the Tories.*
Friday, 4 May 1979. We got the phone on.

I was seventeen and a bit when I wrote that. Knackering up Slabhead's mother's kettle weighed more heavily on me than the leadership spill at Conservative Party head office. As did what I watched on telly, how I got home from night school, which single I wasted 75p on.

But my sympathies lay to the Left, and this allegiance firmed even further during my early working years. At first it was like the hardening of a child's bones as it grows up, an innate process that required no intellectual engagement from me, just as I didn't need to think in order to breathe or for my blood to circulate. The more I read, though, the more I became radicalised.

We got moved around the shipyard so that we were exposed to different types of work and for a while I was in a wee shed inside one of the big hangar-like buildings where the sections of sub were welded together. Our job was to bolt great long heating elements to the hull and pack them with an asbestos substitute in order to pre-heat the metal sections so that they could be welded together without cracking. It wasn't a big shed but there were a few of us in there, and though we all got on there were endless things to argue about: NATO's presence in West Germany, GCHQ, Greenham Common, the dismantling of British Steel. Music was political, with every second gig being a Rock Against Racism fundraiser or some treatise on sexual politics. Even riding a motorbike had its politics.

The Motorcycle Action Group (MAG) had a push for anti-helmet laws and we'd go on rallies, riding around without helmets, sticking it to The Man and doing our best to support organ donation. Some arguments were easy to knock over ('Mrs Thatcher's working class: she works, so she must be') and others not so easy ('You're against nuclear weapons? You seem happy to take home a wage from here every week'). It was a good place to have your views tested. I quickly knew my FSLN from my FMLN and I understood US politics in a way that's since been lost to me, and my sister's Liverpool college was a great source of snarly posters to sit next to Siouxsie Sioux and Pauline Murray.

There was a major debate at the time about whether or not Britain should buy the American Trident submarine system. Opinions for and against filled the news and the pages of the Big Papers and yet, in the shipyard where they'd be built, there was no debate. In the huge sheds where the tumbrels turned night and day to weld the sections of submarine together they were already preparing the jigs for Trident. The cross-sections lay across the shop floor, vast shapes that dwarfed the feeble-looking British subs we were working on. It was a sharp reality check for a young man just beginning to find what I thought was a serious political voice, to discover that in some sense politics is just the background noise to business.

And another thing: with political maturity came those Kuhnian anomalies that soon develop from small cracks into gaping holes in your dearly held theories. The certainty of political allegiance provided a comfort of sorts but the cracks got bigger and, as a teenager with no real foundation in political studies, I struggled to corral all the things that were good within the fold of the Left and ascribe all that was bad to the fascists and Nazis of the Right. I was too stubborn to ever admit that my side of politics could succumb to zealotry and extremism.

Each week during the miners' strike the *Socialist Worker* printed spreads that folded out into posters and I'd put them up in the morning before going out to clag a load more heating elements onto the thick, curved slabs of metal. And every morning when I came back at brew time my foreman, Eddie McAlpine, had torn them down. We had some nose-to-nose, spittle-flying arguments and they always left me nauseous and filled with self-doubt, then angry and filled with self-righteousness afterwards, when I'd thought of all the things I should have said.

I have never voted for anything other than the Left in politics, though my faith has been shaken more times than I care to mention by the careerists and snake-oil merchants that swarm around two-party politics. I often find myself nodding in agreement at some 'independent' or small-party election candidate espousing the protection of domestic manufacturing and the creation of more skilled apprenticeships, only to be brought up sharp when that same candidate segues into a rabid attack on migrants or minorities. I long for that age of blackness and whiteness when everything was so clear to me.

* * *

I was working in one place, a little shed like the pre-heating shed, where we checked stainless steel welds for cracks and flaws. I don't remember much about the process (I wasn't paying too much attention) but there was purple dye that we put on the weld and absorbent strips of paper and a little machine that probably gave us an unsafe dose of radioactive isotopes.

At brew time we would tune the radio in to whatever station was bouncing over the Irish Sea at the time, maybe Manx Radio or something in Welsh or, best of all, an Irish station that had this guy called Larry Gogan. Larry had a segment called *Just a Minute: The Sixty Second Quiz*. I can still sing the jingle. I've since discovered that Larry Gogan is something of a legend, and you can Google pages of daft answers people provided in the heat of answering his seemingly simple questions within the sixty seconds ('A sign of the zodiac? April', 'Something that floats in a bath? Water', 'Hitler's first name? Heil').

I can't imagine working with Larry Gogan but I can imagine working with some of the folk who called in to his show. The place was full of those people called 'characters', a label that covers everyone from the mild eccentric to the rampant psychopath.

Anyone who's lived in a male-only share house will know what can happen when that heady mixture of testosterone, group think and alcohol spits and fizzes and reacts and creates its own microclimate, and the shipyard was like a share house with ten thousand blokes. There were pranks that make *Jackass* look like an under-five's birthday party and each day was like a race to the bottom in taste and morals. Except that there never was a bottom or, if there was, none of us ever found it.

As well as the fact that there were simply too many men in one place, the work culture at the yard was influenced by two critical things: poor management, and an overall sense of the worthlessness of what we were doing. The political Right regularly holds this period up as embodying everything that's wrong with unions, declaring that demarcation and protectionism strangled productivity and innovation. They're wrong about this, for reasons that I can't be bothered to go into now.

The other thing is the thing I want to talk about there, and that was the sense of worthlessness about the work. When I first got out of the apprentice training school and into the yard I was told several times by older workers that the surface vessels and subs we were building would have a life expectancy of about seven minutes in a real conflict. I didn't realise it at the time but this was just the opinion of jaded older guys but I took it as gospel. It seemed plausible enough. The Cold War was in deep permafrost and showed no signs of thawing and the nuclear clock was stuck on three minutes to midnight. Everyone knew that the Russians had a bazillion nuclear warheads and so locking a couple of dozen onto every British vessel ever built seemed like simple maths. Russia *was* the enemy and the only reason that these vessels were being built was to fire off enough explosives back at them before they fired enough off at us to make the possibility of nuclear war unthinkable. So why bother doing your best work on something that'll last seven minutes?

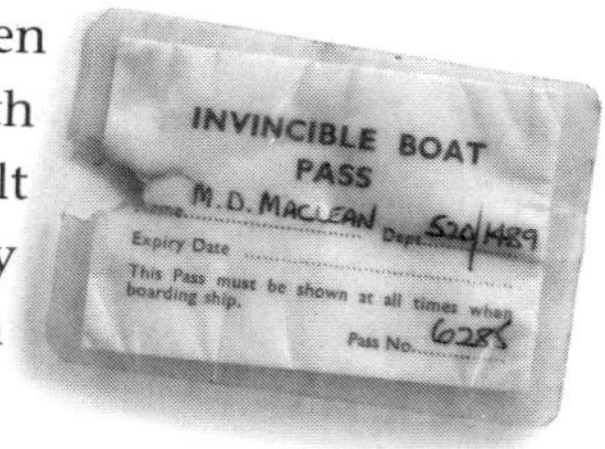

It all came as a bit of a surprise when the war—when it came—wasn't with Russia after all. One of the ships we built was sunk in a time of conflict but not by a dozen missiles launched from a silo in Ukraine; it was sunk by a French-made rocket fired from an Argentine jet over the Falkland Islands. And I remember the hush that fell across the workshop when Danno, whose brother was on the RFA *Sir Tristram*, was called into the foreman's office. It was days before we learned that Danno's brother wasn't at the bottom of Bluff Cove after all but there was a profound change in attitude after that.

A few months later I was down in Liverpool to see my sister and the bus route that took me into town went past the hospital. Through the grime of the bus window I watched a small group of men, about my age. They had Forces' haircuts and sterile bags over the recovering burns where their hands had been and were laughing blackly at their own clumsy attempts to light a cigarette. They didn't look like soldiers or sailors, just like the lads I worked with in the yard, the type of daft kids who'd phone in to Larry Gogan.

* * *

I am really, really surprised to find that I kept scrapbooks. It's kind of quaint.

There are complete articles in there (an article by an American lad called Bill Bryson who looked like he had a bright future ahead of him) but more often than not I've just cut out a picture that's captured my attention and pasted it in: a masked Japanese rioter engulfed in the flames of his own Molotov cocktail, the beheading of a rapist in Jeddah, the bullet-riddled body of Aldo Mori slumped half-in half-out of a car, a group of Kurdish rebels being shot by an Iranian firing squad. All quite ghoulish and graphic. I don't remember sitting down and looking at these pictures once I'd cut them out and pasted them in, yet I must have. What was I thinking as I turned through the heavy black card pages?

There are lots of snippets from the local paper too, the kind of over-the-fence reportage that's so brain-freezingly banal that it can't be anything other than completely hilarious. I've always been attracted to the absurd end of British newspaper reporting and there are dozens of wonderful headlines: 'Man denies throwing curry at shop window', 'Freezer full of fish set on fire in car park' and 'Chip pan fire at boss's home', the latter containing a lovely typo: 'As well as fire damage to electrical appliances, a rubber horse leading to a washing machine also burned through causing a small flood in the house.'

There are cartoons, mostly the snarky Left-wing stuff that the *Guardian* specialised in and that I'd come to appreciate. As a kid I'd always thought of cartoons as things that were funny, or at least had a punchline. I'd grown up with the *Beano*, my cousin getting the *Dandy*. We'd swap on the weekend but I always felt like he was getting the best end of the deal; the *Beano* had the Bash Street Kids and General Jumbo and Dennis the Menace whereas the Dandy felt lame and olden times: Minnie the Minx and Winker Watson and that sheep dog, though Bully Beef and Chips was OK. When I graduated to grown-up papers it was Andy Capp and The Perishers in the *Mirror* and Hagar the Horrible in the *Sun*. None of them ever actually made me laugh and yet, for years, I expected (and was endlessly disappointed not to get) a chuckle.

These *Guardian* cartoons weren't like that. Everything about the way they looked gave the impression of funniness in the offing but they were more about social commentary and reinforcing the siege mentality that was creeping over the Left after the Falklands War. You didn't see the 'Don't blame me: I voted Labour' badges after 1982, and the more entrenched in government that the Right became the crankier and less funny the Left became. As a rule I think the Left does its best satire from opposition; triumphalism and crowing sits uncomfortably with socialism and is best left to the Right. But those years were a wilderness for Leftist humour; there was a shouty anger to it that made me uneasy.

I thought at the time that I was falling out of love with the Left but I was just growing up a bit. I don't mean that I was softening and my politics were moving to the Right but I was starting to develop a suspicion of the clubiness that was part of the deal of being on any side of politics. I'm sure I would have liked Nancy Banks Smith and the rest of the *Guardian* contributors if I'd met them, but I knew in my heart that I never would, ever. They belonged to a branch of the Left that lived on a different planet to mine; rightly or wrongly I scented privilege and education and betterment, and me, with my whopping great chip weighing heavily on my shoulder, didn't like that smell. I imagined them as the people who cut their sandwiches in triangles and used the front door, who had 'dinner' rather than 'tea', who wouldn't know a can of Swarfega from an avocado dip. I was growing up.

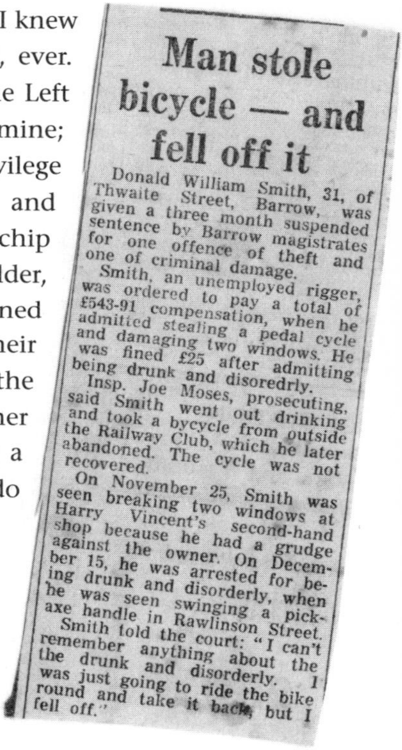

Man stole bicycle — and fell off it

Donald William Smith, 31, of Thwaite Street, Barrow, was given a three month suspended sentence by Barrow magistrates for one offence of theft and one of criminal damage.

Smith, an unemployed rigger, was ordered to pay a total of £543-91 compensation, when he admitted stealing a pedal cycle and damaging two windows. He was fined £25 after admitting being drunk and disoredrly.

Insp. Joe Moses, prosecuting, said Smith went out drinking and took a bycycle from outside the Railway Club, which he later abandoned. The cycle was not recovered.

On November 25, Smith was seen breaking two windows at Harry Vincent's second-hand shop because he had a grudge against the owner. On December 15, he was arrested for being drunk and disorderly, when he was seen swinging a pick-axe handle in Rawlinson Street.

Smith told the court: "I can't remember anything about the drunk and disorderly. I was just going to ride the bike round and take it back, but I fell off."

PARLOPHONE
DOWNTOWN
PETULA CLARK
TONY HATCH
45RPM
TRADEMARK OF

Box 4

We were out one Friday night, in a fancy bar in the east end of town. I was drinking a 'craft' beer, which is the name for a beer that doesn't give you much change out of a tenner and comes in a disappointingly small glass and doesn't necessarily taste like beer. We were talking about our favourite authors of all time. By the time you get to my age (he says, running his thumbs down the insides of his braces and stretching them away from his soft paunch) you don't have definitive favourites any more: everything starts to become a mixture of whatever you've already experienced. If my kids play new music I tend to say, 'Oh, they're not bad. They're a bit like XYZ, with a bit of ABC thrown in.' Which of course drives them nuts. No, they snarl back at me, they're not in the least bit like XYZABC; they *are* . . . whoever they *are*.

There's also the ability to feel, which diminishes as you get older. (Apparently. My kids have told me so.) I remember seeing *Apocalypse Now* in 1979 and stumbling mute from the cinema, such was its effect on me. Now, I'd probably say, 'Oh, it was all right. Kind of like *Bridge over the River Kwai*, with a bit of *Blue Velvet* thrown in.'

My first favourite author was Enid Blyton. I had all twenty-one of the Famous Five books but there is not one Enid Blyton book in the whole five boxes.

The next author I was mad for was Arthur Ransome; the twelve *Swallows and Amazons* books are all there. I didn't understand *Swallows and Amazons* to begin with. That opening section of the first book, with Roger tacking into the wind up the hillside to deliver the telegram to Mummy might as well

have been written in Hebrew. What *is* tacking? And that message about duffers not drowning? And can there really be people in the world called Titty? I didn't get it and so I didn't try to read it again till I was maybe thirteen. After that, I ripped through the lot of them.

After this there was a kind of zigzag period when I read anything from Hammond Innes to Dennis Wheatley. Then in my mid to late teens there were a few authors whose books blew me away, specifically Jack Kerouac (because he was completely bonkers) and Voltaire (because it was the first time I realised that people in the olden days had a sense of humour). After that there were lots of books that were 'classics', which I knew them to be because of the clue word 'classic' on the cover, even if they were often really boring or hard to understand: Jean Genet, Gabriel Chevallier, LP Hartley, Daphne du Maurier. But the two authors that define that period are Franz Kafka and PG Wodehouse, which sums me up as a darkly introspective optimist who liked a giggle.

Some of them I never owned. In fact, a good part of my book learning came from a higher authority: my sister.

* * *

My sister is five years older than me. She is one of the most focused, intelligent, determined, hardworking and disciplined people I've ever come across. I don't know how my parents created her, which sounds worse than it's meant to. I mean, my parents aren't idiots, but my sister is just one out of the box. A mould-breaker. Mam and Dad must have thought that the whole parenting thing was a doddle: you simply made a baby and off it went, charging through life, tackling one thing after another, achieving, doing, making, improving.

And then they had me. It'd be enough to take the wind out of anyone's sails. I can imagine them worrying, asking those sly questions of other parents about the stages of development ('When do you think it's all right for a boy to stop rubbing rice pudding onto his head?'). I don't want to overstate the case, but it must have knocked their confidence. I was an idler, a dreamer, easily distracted by the jingle of keys or the glint of sunlight on milk bottle tops.

My sister did well in her A Levels and was now off at teacher-training college in Liverpool. At the end of school I'd been given forms for various courses in further education but I knew that this was not going to happen. Mam and Dad weren't trying to stifle my future by commanding me to get a trade; as far as they were concerned it was the path to liberation.

For the last few years of my schooling and the first of my apprenticeship I would get the train down to Liverpool and camp out at my sister's place. I'd go to Anfield to watch the football or go out to clubs in Toxteth, the haze of dope so thick in the air it made your eyes smart, or hang around the legendary record shops in town. I must have looked (to her, at least) to be in need of direction, or maybe she didn't have enough on her plate already. Either way, she took me on as a project.

I know this because of the letters. I'd completely forgotten that we wrote to each other until I came across them. It seems like such a strange and remote thing to do in these days of Snapchat and the Facebook message: brothers and sisters picking up pen and paper and writing letters to each other. I haven't got my end of the correspondence but in hers there's talk about how her teaching's going, or directions for me to get to the latest flat, or what I should bring down from home. (I still remember lugging a massive red vacuum cleaner across Preston Station.)

And reading lists. Extracts from various letters indicate the range of her ambitions for me:

> *As you enjoyed* Room at the Top, This Sporting Life *is in the same vein – read it with the local rugby in mind.*
> *Another excellent John Wyndham for you. I'll bring some short stories up next time.*
> *I find JP Donleavy ridiculous and very funny, I like his verbosity and richness of words – very funny too. Have you read the Brendan Behan yet?*
> *Nancy Mitford is hilarious, to be read for pure enjoyment.*
> *The Evelyn Waugh is the 2nd in a trilogy and unfortunately I don't yet have the other two. He is a 1930's contemporary of Nancy Mitford and in my opinion balances well, showing the* <u>other</u> *side of the rich life. Read Scott Fitzgerald (*Precious is the Night *etc.) for this too.*
> *I have some Alec Waugh at home, he is brother to Evelyn and either uncle or father to Auberon.*
> *I'll bring you some more Graham Greene.*
> *P.S. Put the plastic cover on when you take them to work.*

Oh yes, put the plastic cover on when you take them to work. So when everyone else is checking out the tits in the *Sun* and the *Star*, I can delve into my plastic-covered copy of *The Outsider* or *The Anti-Death League*.

I might have looked like a right pompous git, but I wasn't the only one who was Improving.

* * *

The shipyard was full of people like Big Peter, who was studying Anglo-Saxon literature through the Open University and spent his brew time translating the Anglo-Saxon Chronicles. There was Jerry Tange, a bearded shop steward who never did anything resembling work but was plodding through a psychology degree. Specialists in local history were ten a penny, as were students of the railway systems of the Commonwealth or linguistic morphology or genetics. All these autodidacts, quietly improving themselves.

It must have been about 1980 that I started studying anthropology. I saw a roneo-ed poster in the town library advertising night school courses through the Workers Education Authority. Quite what appealed to me about it I don't know, but I mentioned it at the pub and another lad, Dennis Tyson, enrolled with me. Dennis was a year or two older, worked at the slipper factory and loved a smoke, so I think he must have felt the need to expand his consciousness in other ways. We signed up, the two of us, to a great deal of good-natured piss-taking from everyone in the front bar.

It was held on a Tuesday in a town about six miles away, over the fells. I had a two-stroke Yamaha trail bike at the time and I'd pick Dennis up and off we'd go, up and over the tops. It was a particularly wet, cold winter and the two of us got flogged with rain, sleet and hail the whole way there and back, and yet still we turned up. We were the odd couple. The lecturer was this *really* old guy (that is, in his late thirties or early forties) who may or may not have been an anthropologist. These days I've got friends whose fathers research topics such as Wagner's Ring Cycle or Captain Cook's observation of the eclipse at the Tropic of Capricorn and then deliver lectures on the subject at U3A, but at the time I just assumed that someone sitting at the front of a class was an expert on a topic simply by virtue of their sitting with the blackboard behind them.

It was an entry-level course but I thought, 'This is all right.' And something else: I understood it. I got it. If I'd learnt anything from school and then the night schools and block releases of my apprenticeship it was that I wasn't good at it; I didn't get it. I could study Electrical Applications (Heavy) for a year and none of it seemed to stick; this stuff stuck after one night. And so I began to think about thinking.

* * *

These LP records and seven-inch singles: who would have thought they weighed so much? When I was packing the boxes in England there was a limit of 35 kilograms per box and a stack of LPs took that up in no time.

Leaving home was a gradual process, like the small tugs you make when you're pulling off a Band-Aid. It takes a few half-hearted attempts until you realise that it's going to hurt less if you get it over with in a single swipe. I can gauge when those first tentative tugs started—the point at which I found myself living in share houses and grotty digs—by the ratio of LPs to cassettes. I got a Walkman around 1981 and it became easier to throw a couple of dozen tapes into a bag than cart a stack of LPs and a turntable around the country. So these bits of vinyl date from around 1976 to 1982 or '83.

The LPs now sit in a stack, leaning face out against the wall of my office. They look so few, such a puny collection. There *were* more, I know. There are lots missing—all the ones from the pre-punk days, the Black Sabbath and Led Zeppelin, The Who and (blush) Hot Chocolate. The bootlegs: Stranglers, Siouxsie and the Banshees, Patti Smith. They've gone the way of all records: lost, or lent and never returned, or warped and thrown out, or sold on eBay. (Same as the Typhoo Tea card albums: Where did they all go?)

It's a while before I dig out the turntable from the shed, and a while more before I can face cleaning it of the dust and filth and cockroach poo that covers everything in those dark recesses. It's just a turntable though; there's no amp. A local music store sells me a thing called a pre-amp, whatever that is, and then I have to get a new needle. I go down to the second-hand bookshop that also has a big record collection. I tell the man the model of the turntable and the man tells me that he doesn't stock that particular needle, but he has a contact who does. Doris has needles for all turntables. She is the Needle Lady. He rings Doris and when he talks to her he kind of covers the telephone receiver with his hand as though he doesn't want me to overhear their conversation. It's over in a few seconds anyway; he puts the phone down and tells me that Doris will drop off a needle next Wednesday. I turn up early, hoping to meet Doris. I've got a picture of her in my head: Doris the Needle Lady. But she's too wily for me; even though I'm there at opening time the man tells me that she's already been and gone. I part with the $36 and scuttle home, disappointed and excited at the same time.

I get everything plugged in and sorted and then look at my records. Where to start? I pick out a single at random: The Cramps, *Fever*. It's amazing! All the cracks and hisses and pops that people talk about, the *soul* of vinyl, it's there! I up the speakers so that I can feel Poison Ivy's thumping bass. I'm looking at the single's picture cover and reading all the notes and details and I'm just getting into it when, after less than three and a half minutes, it's over. I turn the single over and play the B side, *Garbageman*. Again, brilliant! Again, over in three and a half minutes. I have to get up again. Bloody hell. I haven't got time for this. It strikes me that I must have spent half of my teenage years getting up and down again just to change records.

Within three more singles I've realised why there are no record shops any more. Sure, those LP sleeves with their liner notes are lovely. I haven't played or even held records for decades and so it's a wild pleasure when I slide out a record from its sleeve and find an inside sleeve that I'd forgotten about: the pictures on Elvis Costello's *This Year's Model*, the photo sheet on Fleetwood Mac's *Rumours*, the lyrics sheet on Talking Heads' *Speaking in Tongues*. And coloured vinyl! What a surprise to slide Television's *Adventure* and find that it's on red vinyl!

But all that getting up and down again. Who can be bothered?

* * *

My son wanders into the kitchen ready to go out for the night. He's got on a Ben Sherman T-shirt, the one with the British Air Force roundel, and a green parka and straight-leg jeans. I say, 'Wait there!' and run out to my office and get my copy of The Who's *Quadraphenia* and open up the double-album spread to show him the photographic essay that came pasted inside every copy. As I turn the heavy paper pages I see a version of him on every page but he . . .

Well, he looks at it with the listless, wary eye of a teenager. He doesn't want to appear positive or enthusiastic because this might encourage me in some way, fuel that misguided, needy part of the parent that wants to *connect* with the child. He maybe mutters 'Cool' in a neutral way, the equivalent of tousling my hair and giving me a cheerful wink.

What did I expect? This double album with its fancy artwork and its photos of kids that dressed as he's dressing now but forty years earlier: it's just a source to him. This is the generation that draws on sources like no other has before. Want to form a band with Motown influences? YouTube it. Can't make out that song lyric? Google it. Want to know who Gene Krupa was? Wikipedia. Everything is out there, immediate and available. And the tribes? Forget about it. The tribal identities my friends and I displayed through our clothes and music and attitudes: are they still there? I don't think cosplay fiends get into street battles with lumbersexuals. It's all gone.

* * *

The family record player was a little blue and white thing that closed up like a briefcase. It had an adaptor for those records with big holes in the centre, and played at four speeds: 16 rpm, 33, 45 and 78. I don't think we owned any 16 rpm records but it was quite hilarious turning Mam's Frank Sinatra up to 78 then down to 16, usually accompanied by frenzied sped-up dancing followed by slow, zombie-like staggering around the room.

As a teenager I was pretty snooty about Norma's records but, compared to the records I started buying, it was a bloody great collection. Norma hit thirty in the mid Sixties and so she was still young when the Beatles, the Stones, Dylan and the Motown juggernaut rumbled over the world. Among her favourites were songs like The Who's *I Can See for Miles* and Dylan's *Rainy Day Woman #12 and 35*. I can never listen to Petula Clark's *Downtown* without hearing the peculiar throaty cough of the vinyl scratch that accompanied Tony Hatch's introductory piano. She had some crap too, chief amongst which was Richard Harris's *Macarthur Park*.

I love the paper sleeves and the coloured labels, none of which match because of endless pulling out and playing and

replacing. The hot pink-and-black print of the Pye label for *Downtown.* The Yardbirds' *For Your Love* is inside a Decca sleeve that's orange with vertical white pinstripes, with a graphic of an ear and the words 'full frequency range recording: true high fidelity'. The Supremes' *You Keep Me Hangin' On* (black Tamla Motown label with grey text) in a peppermint green Columbia sleeve with white dots on the sidebar and, on the reverse adverts for E.M.I. record tokens (From 6 shillings to 50 shillings: for the 'present' and the future). Gladys Knight and the Pips' *Help Me Make It Through the Night* on Tamla Motown in a dark green Parlaphone sleeve with an advert on the back for *Record Mail,* 'A lively illustrated Monthly Review of the latest "POPS". Full of pictures and information about your favourite artists.' Richard Harris's *Macarthur Park* on RCA Victor in a claret Capitol sleeve, with on the back adverts for 'The best of . . .' series of LPs, including Gene Vincent, Peggy Lee, Dean Martin, Nat King Cole and Frank Sinatra. Len Barry's *1–2–3* on Brunswick.

* * *

I've been doing a bit of teaching, high school History. When I talk about the grand arc of history, as I'm wont to do, I mention to the kids something that I think is mind-boggling: that Cleopatra is closer in time to us than she is to the building of the pyramids; that Tyrannosaurus Rex is closer in time to us than to Stegosaurus; that . . . well, as Yul Brynner would say in *The King and I,* et cetera, et cetera, et cetera. Then something odd happens. The thing that thrills me about history and makes me go all tingly has absolutely no effect on the students, other than making them want to check their phones under the desk or slump face forward in a stupor of boredom.

How can the back and forth of time not be endlessly fascinating? Gripping?

As apprentices we were put to work under the guidance of senior tradesmen called journeymen. (Which has always

puzzled me. A 'journeyman footballer' is one who's not bad, but not all that great; does that mean that we were taught by tradesmen who were not bad, but not all that great?) One of my first journeymen was a bloke called Danny Coulthard, who seemed old, but not one-foot-in-the-grave ancient. Danny didn't talk about it much but occasional stories about the war would emerge, in the way that people mention something that happened to them when they were teenagers. The time he leaned over to pick up an orange and the sniper's bullet that was meant for him took out his mate behind him, or the time he wet his pants when being strafed by a Stuka while waiting to be evacuated from Dunkirk. Another journeyman, Ernie, had been an ambulance driver in the war and reckoned the beach at Anzio was the worst thing he ever saw. And another, Don, saw plenty of action but thought that the starved orphans living in the rubble of post-liberation Berlin was worse. All these guys were close to retirement at the time, so they were oldish, but not *that* old. The war had finished just over thirty years before, so if Don was twenty in Berlin he'd have been about the age I am now when I was his apprentice.

And yet the war, and soldiering in general, was something that you put behind you. I guess it was a process they learnt from the generation before: you were called, you went, and upon your return you picked up where you'd left off. Don't go on about it because we were all in the same boat and, frankly, no one's interested.

Well I was. And a generation of kids that bought comics like *Commando, Victor* and *Battle* were too. Each week a raggedy but stoic bunch of Tommies would overcome insurmountable odds to defeat a troop of ruthless, robot-like Nazis or shrill, fanatic Japs. We lapped it up, even when the stories were blatantly moralistic in tone ('Gunner Smith had always been a loner, shunned by the brigade, until a chance discovery in a muddy French field changed everything. But at what cost?').

I was thumbing through a copy of *Planet of the Apes* (#21 as a matter of fact, week ending March 15, 1975, price 8p) with the intention of writing something about the covers. Issue 1 had a very realistic painting of a bearded human who is being lassoed by an ape mounted on a horse, but this was an aberration and all the covers afterwards have the standard Marvel drawing style. I always felt a bit cheated by that. Anyway, as well as changing drawing styles I think they must have run out of man versus ape ideas because, in issue 21, we've moved on to 'Monster vs. Ape! In a world gone mad!' and in an 'Evolution nightmare' we're introduced to *Killdozer!*, a kind of precursor of *Christine*, the mad Plymouth Fury in the film of the same name. Killdozer makes sounds like *Skreeeeee!* and *Spabooom!* and *Zzzzraaaakkkk!*

And, on page 11, is this advert for The Airfix Gang.

The johnnies in the advertising room at Airfix Central (I can picture it in my mind) were no slouches. Rather than stick a half-page box ad in with pictures of Airfix models and a snappy slogan such as *Children of Britain: Buy Airfix products!*, they've thought about their comic-buying audience and created their own 'action' strip. Poor Alan wants to be in The Airfix Gang but his models aren't up to scratch. Off he goes to his local toyshop, where a pipe-smoking gentleman sells him a proper Airfix kit, which has 'accuracy, better reproduction and more realistic moving parts'. At home he has lots of fun building the kit . . . until his dad joins in. 'I used to fly in the war blah blah blah' says the text in the speech bubble.

I can see what they were trying to do; a mid Seventies version of being 'down' with the kids. But, bookended as it is by *Killdozer!* and *Death Lies at the Mountain of Madness,* the Airfix ad looks, reads and feels totally weak in a particularly British way. It was the 'blah blah blah' that made life interesting. My History teacher at secondary school had no formal qualifications that I could make out other than that he'd fought his way through North Africa and Italy, liked olden times things and ran the model club on Friday after school. He was easily among the worst teachers I've eve had. His lessons involved him reading out of a textbook in a dull monotone and us going like the clappers to write everything down, refilling fountain pens with ink and, at the end, shaking our numbed hands to regain circulation. But during model club, as we glued bits of a de Havilland Mosquito to our fingertips, Harry would talk about the war and became a different man, an orator who held us entranced with the stories of the ancient riches he saw in the bombed out churches of southern Italy.

There were still bomb sites in town, terraced streets that ended abruptly in a block of waste ground with thistles and piles of bricks turned into bike ramps. On the gable ends you could see the soot line from where the chimney had been in the house that was no longer there. It was not that long ago, close enough in time to almost touch.

* * *

Much of my very early listening relied on the records in the house. There were Scottish folk songs, such as the *Mingulay Boat Song,* on 78s. I think there was a copy of *The Good, the Bad and the Ugly,* which was probably my sister's.

As I matured a little I delved into her records; she was of the age when troubadours like Ralph McTell, Don McLean,

Donovan, Rory Gallagher and Elton John ruled the airwaves. She had cassettes of *Tapestry* and *The Best of the Jackson 5*. After a trip to France she came back with exotic Jacques Brel records, and after a trip to the USA came back with Jim Croce.

I was never one for the balladeers but didn't yet know what I did like. After I got a Sunday paper round I had a little disposable income and started buying cassettes to play on my sister's player. *Houses of the Holy* by Led Zeppelin, for no other reason than that I liked the cover and I'd heard of them. You would think, given that my cash was so hard-earned, I'd have been more discriminating in my buying but I wasn't. I bought Black Sabbath, only to realise that I didn't like them, and Pink Floyd's *Animals*, surely one of the worst records ever made. But I did like the cover. I bought the first four Roxy Music albums from a second-hand shop on the basis of a couple of songs I knew and those brilliant covers.

* * *

The suburbs: the despised, reviled suburbs. The Seventies hated the suburbs more than any other decade. People who lived in the suburbs were the fodder of dozens of lame British sitcoms. The whole punk thing was about hating the suburbs, because of course all punks lived in council houses and squats. But, oh God, how I longed to live in the suburbs—anything but this pebble-dashed bungalow in the countryside with its allotment next door.

The exoticness of the suburbs was entirely due to their mystery. I had no idea really what a suburb was. The nearest big town had different 'parts' like Hawcoat, Strawberry, Newbarns, Ormsgill and so on. But I don't think they were suburbs. No one ever said, 'I'm from the suburb of Ormsgill, the one next to the slaggies.'

Suburbs were places where people led double lives, they were inhabited by suited men who worked in offices in the city (or maybe The City) and they commuted on trains with briefcases and umbrellas in their hands, leaving behind their frustrated and steamy wives to answer the door to the milkman in their slinky negligees.

* * *

I'm listening to the Sex Pistols single *Pretty Vacant*. It's not bad: a bit angry and shouty and quite a lot of fun. It's got that brilliant closing line that sums up the punk attitude and would make all the vicars and councillors and *Daily Mail* letter writers apoplectic: *And we don't care!* Love it.

The outrage that swept Britain with the arrival of the Pistols seems almost quaint now; we look back on it and allow ourselves a sophisticated chuckle in the same way that we pity those buttoned-up folk in the Fifties who thought that if Elvis Presley gyrated his hips on TV every teenage girl in Alabama would fall pregnant. I remember the thrill of buying *God Save the Queen*, and the withering look the woman behind the counter gave me. Maybe if I'd bought it in a groovy record shop in a big city I'd have had a different experience, but I bought it upstairs at Quilliam's Electrical. There were a couple of specialist record shops in town, there was one that even had the old-style listening booths with headphones, but most places that sold records were electrical stores that had made a bit of space upstairs. (It was always upstairs.) Friths' was a hardware shop where you could still buy a quarter pound of black-japanned woodscrews and the man scooped them into a paper bag and weighed them out. And yet, bizarrely, they also sold Sex Pistols records. Upstairs. And Boots the chemist had a spot, next to where you got your films developed. Upstairs.

Interviews with punk bands always bang on about the bleak and parlous state of Britain at the time: bin men on strike,

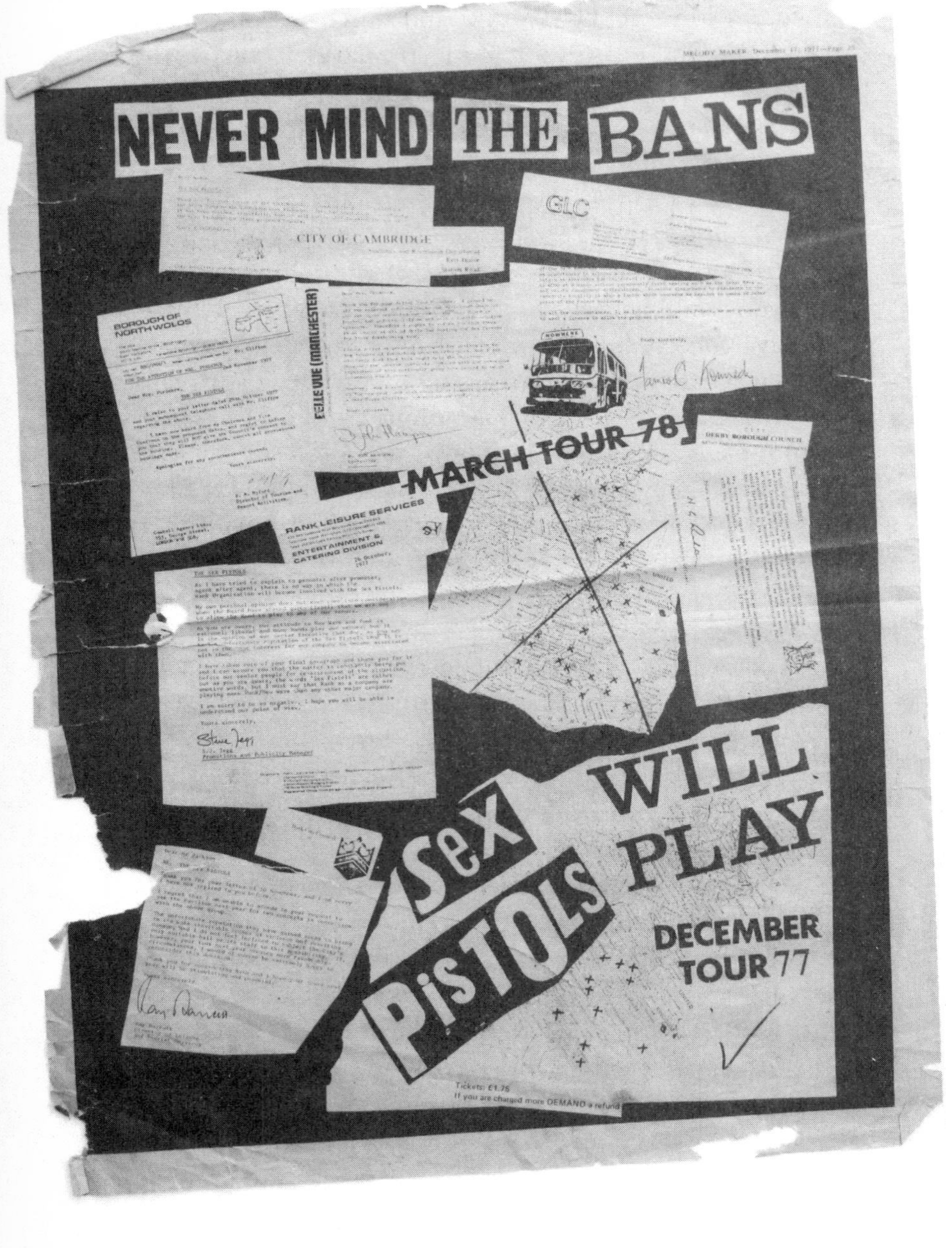

MELODY MAKER, December 17, 1977
NEVER MIND THE BANS
CITY OF CAMBRIDGE
GLC
BOROUGH OF NORTHWOLDS
BELLE VUE (MANCHESTER)
NOWHERE
MARCH TOUR 78
DERBY BOROUGH COUNCIL
RANK LEISURE SERVICES
ENTERTAINMENT & CATERING DIVISION
THE SEX PISTOLS
SEX PISTOLS WILL PLAY
DECEMBER TOUR 77
Tickets: £1.75
If you are charged more DEMAND a refund

gravediggers on strike, miners on strike. Pictures of London show the streets lined with piles and piles of uncollected black bin bags. The place was going to the dogs. It sounds awful, and it bears no resemblance whatsoever to my memory of the time. I was having a ball, running around in the sunshine and getting a lovely tan, learning to sight and shoot an air rifle properly, trying to get served in pubs, riding my mate's Suzuki trail bike in the sand hills.

And I was up and down the fells and on the shore and in the woods building up my collection of birds' eggs. It wasn't a massive collection but it wasn't bad. I started off with a tray filled with sawdust and the eggs sat in rows, then when it outgrew the tray my dad made me a proper box and got some fine sawdust from a timber yard. It looked great and I'd look at them for hours, turning them over and examining their mottled detail. Each one had its own story: the curlew's egg from amongst the heather on the tops overlooking the estuary; the blue tit's egg from its nest in a dry-stone wall; the lapwing's egg from the reedy marshland that flooded every winter.

You might remember that I was in the YOC at the time as well, and would go off bird-watching and spend weekends on sponsored bird-watches and tick off sightings in my *Observer's Book of Birds*. And yet I'd also tick off the eggs in my *Observer's Book of Birds Eggs*; in fact, I just noticed that on the title page of the *Observer's Book of Birds Eggs* I've written my name followed by my YOC membership number. It sounds like I should have been more conflicted by this than I was. You're probably expecting me, in the story that follows, to lay out for you my moment on the road to Damascus when the horror and realisation of what I was doing hit me four-square in the head and changed me forever. It didn't.

Something happened, but not in a rumble of thunder and flash of lightning way. It was more the growing awareness and disquietude of some hard-to-pin-down anomaly. Alfred and Edith in Jonathan Franzen's *The Corrections* hear it as the alarm of anxiety, a far-distant klaxon that no one else appears to be aware of. Anxiety might be overstating it but the maturing period of those mid-teen years did trigger a raising of my head from my navel and the desire to start looking at the world around me. A sense of place and belonging is important at any time of life but in adolescence it assumes an importance that pales in adulthood. The *Who am I?* and *Where do I belong?* questions are for most of us not yet clearly answered. I played *Pretty Vacant* on the turntable in our house, conscious of the fact that I didn't live in a crumbling council house in an urban jungle. I lived in a pebble-dashed bungalow that my dad had built. The broken, piss-stinking elevator belonged to the world of TV shows like *The Sweeney*; I don't think I'd actually even been in a lift at that point in my life; the nearest thing was the escalator at Tesco in town (which only went up, you had to get the stairs back down again), which as littler kids we'd spend Saturday afternoons going up and up and up on until the cranky store manager chucked us out.

The eggs thing started to nag at me a bit. I maybe I felt some shame, even while I continued to raid nests and blow the yolks and nestle the shells into place in the smooth sawdust. The collecting of the eggs was just an end point in a process; the real thing was in the countless hours spent observing bird behaviour and in getting to know what habitat might attract what species under what circumstances. Having an egg collection was part of the same circle as the desire to know the birds themselves, a knowledge that (to my mind at the time) could not be gained simply by reading books or watching David Attenborough documentaries or even sitting in a hide with a pair of binoculars. I had to be up that tree, in that marsh, wading through that waist-high purple heather.

I sound like an apologist. People who are against duck shooters will never be able to fathom the shooters' concept of themselves as nature's custodians, and hunt saboteurs will never understand the fox-hunters' self-image as guardians of the countryside. I'm not sure it's purely a countryside thing as there are plenty of people from the countryside who despise fox hunting and duck shooting—and egg collecting. But to this day it's a liminal zone in my mind.

When I left school and started work I joined the union. Even if there'd been a choice about it, which there wasn't, I would have done so. It was natural to be a part of the collective. The semi-mechanised hay-timing that took place around the village when I was a youngster was an all-hands-to-the-pump approach, with everyone in the fields, women driving tractors and men throwing rectangular bales onto trailers and us kids getting in the way. But we were being inculcated with an understanding of how collective, task-oriented work happens. The collective good wasn't a philosophy, it was a living necessity. If we thought of ourselves as having a class then its name was 'working', regardless of whether or not this meshed with Marxist theory. We knew we were different to the working class of the towns and cities in Carlisle and Manchester. We were tribal with no tribe.

The shipyard was the polar opposite to the task-oriented world of the fields that lay but a few miles from its centre; the yard was time-oriented to the nearest second. When the clocking-on machine went with a dull thunk from 7.30 to 7.31 and the ribbon changed from black to red. If you were working, at nine o'clock you dropped your banding tool midway through strapping up some cables because it was brew time, and no one worked between 9.01 and 9.10.

As I became a little older I began to engage more closely with politics. My sensibilities lay to the Left and so that's where I gravitated to. But it was not without some reluctance. Though the Left more clearly articulated my rural sense that the good of the collective outweighs the good of the individual I also had something of the rural libertarian in me—with its inherent suspicion of the city-dweller.

It's nothing new: city versus country; individual versus collective; council house versus pebble-dashed bungalow. I didn't ever get to see the wine bars full of chinless toffs chugging their City bonuses that apparently characterised the Eighties. It just didn't happen like that round our way, or around the way of 99 per cent of Britain. That social and political lurch to the Right that took place during the time I'm remembering has, if anything, helped to clarify in my mind those areas of politics and ethics that were still clouded for me in 1978. I like to think that the teenage me would be comforted by the fact that I'm angrier now than I've ever been about the way in which the Right has privatised our collective wealth while nationalising the greed-driven losses that inevitably occur when they over-reach themselves. He might be surprised to hear that I'm still ambivalent about the killing of ducks and foxes, and pine for that egg collection that was stored in the attic until it was eaten by mice.

I still like the riotous anger of *Pretty Vacant* and I still think that Rotten's sneering *And we don't care!* sums up punk to perfection and I still like to think I've got some of that punk attitude. But—I felt it at the time and I feel it still—I could never buy in completely. Not because I was 'the only punk in the village' or because I didn't live on a piss-stinking council estate—I mean that I couldn't buy in completely to everything: the Left, the Right, the city, the punk movement, the union. Perhaps those hours and hours of running around stubble fields amongst people who were grafting like blazes to get a harvest in rubbed off on my DNA. Or maybe it's the selfish isolation of the egg collector that makes me suspicious of the collective. Or . . . I don't know. Even after all these years I don't have an answer to it.

* * *

I'm listening to The Pretenders' first LP. Play side one, turn it over and play side two, turn it over and play side one again. It's not so bad after all, the getting up and down every now and again. Maybe not for singles but LPs are all right. And for a gentleman of a certain age who leads a sedentary lifestyle it could be just the ticket to a new, healthier me.

But what a lot of rubbish LPs I own! We call them 'record collections' but this one looks thrown together. Three Dead Kennedys albums and two Vibrators albums? They're all right, the Kennedys, in that West Coast surf-punk kind of way but once you've been hit with the punchline it doesn't really change from song to song. And the Vibrators? I didn't think I had anything at all of theirs, let alone two LPs. Are they someone else's? Did I borrow them and not return them? Am I that bad person?

* * *

Is there anything or anyone more indignant than a teenager whose artfully constructed universe of rebellion is being challenged by the stupefyingly dull forces of The Establishment, as personified by his parents?

If The Stranglers song *Peaches* is discussed at all it's usually in reference to the lyrics, particularly the word 'clitoris', which the fusty old nobs at the BBC didn't understand (so the story goes), in the same way that they didn't know what 'giving head' meant when Lou Reed sang *Walk on the Wild Side* on *Top of the Pops*. Who cares. (Nobody was 'giving head' in Cumbria back then anyway; it was called 'getting sucked off'. Which sounds horrible. If there's going to be a right way of describing it then perhaps the Yanks got it right.) My memory of the lyrics to *Peaches* is the bit about the skewer ('I could think of a lot worse places to be / Like down on the street / Or down in the sewer / Or even on the end of a skewer!').

It made our Mam laugh like a drain, which she could do when the circumstances were right. If you say that someone 'threw back their heads and laughed' it sounds more like a stage direction or a line in a book, but Norma sure did when she heard that line. At which point I, of course, got all haughty and started blustering something or other to do with how brilliant punk was, all the while getting a bit red-faced because deep down I think I knew it was indeed a truly daft lyric. And my bluster made our Mam try to stop laughing, because none of us deliberately mock our own children, but then she'd look at me and burst out into more hysterics.

I said that parents don't deliberately mock their children but I do have quite a few memories of Mam having a good laugh at my expense. I remember coming home from town with an extremely special early Eighties a la mode haircut; once again, Mam threw her head back and had a good old chortle. 'You look like Stan Laurel!' she finally managed once she'd got her voice back. Another time, drunk, I was completely unable to undo the laces of my Doc Martens. I remember her standing in the doorway of my bedroom while I picked feebly at this tight wet knot and chuntered on about 'Big Brother is watching', while she creased up.

She's been dead a good few years now and I still think about her and yet I'd forgotten about how we'd tease each other to the point where one of us would get cranky and the other would pretend to look all repentant, then the cranky-looking one would feel the overwhelming desire to start laughing, which would make the other one start laughing too.

I hardly ever laughed like this with Dad. Not that he wasn't funny, we just didn't laugh that way. And yet he occupies my memories in a way that poor old Norma doesn't just because he's still alive and she isn't. As time goes by her ability to fill the spaces of my imagination and memory recedes.

I feel like I'm losing her in some way, and the stuff reminds me of what it was that I've lost.

* * *

When they haul people out of the audience to be contestants on *RocKwiz*, Julia Zemiro will ask them a series of questions to introduce them to us viewers at home. The questions 'What was the first record you bought?' and 'What was the first concert you ever went to?' are perennial icebreakers. Like my first kiss, I can't honestly remember the first record I bought. It might have been that Led Zeppelin cassette, or some dud single like *Jeans On* by David Dundas, which still lurks at the back of the collection. I can answer the 'first concert' question with more authority though: Thin Lizzy at the Liverpool Empire.

It was an early birthday present from my sister. She was at teacher-training college in Liverpool and I went down after school one weekend. I don't remember being a Thin Lizzy fan beforehand, so I'm not sure why she picked them for me, but I sure was a fan afterwards. They sat alongside The Who as favourites until the tectonic shift of punk.

Except that it isn't true. The first band I ever really saw, the first group of people who sang and played instruments together, was a Christian collective called Certain Sounds.

They played at our school in 1974 or 1975, loose West Coast harmonies with an overarching 'God is good' and 'We are all special in His eyes' theme. Why did they bother coming to my dead-end corner of England? Had they been lectured about the heathen Cumbrian children at their Sunday schools? I have no answer to these questions. But they were American and, in the mid Seventies, being American was enough to make you massively *massively* cool. Me and my friends thought they were brilliant, and when one friend's dad (the one with the Commander Gordon red telephone in the hallway) said he'd take us to the nearest Big Town to see them perform in a drafty church hall we jumped at the chance. So not only were they the first band I ever saw, they were also the second. They'd have been the third too if I'd have had my way.

Within three years I was a different person, the kind of person who would have spat on Certain Sounds in the street, or at least curled my lip and sneered at them in such a way as to send them all scuttling back to the Carolinas.

* * *

The middle 1970s were brilliant—literally. I had this salmon and pink paisley patterned shirt and I was by no means the most flamboyant dresser in my group. On Thursday nights on *Top of the Pops* you might see Roxy Music or Sweet or Slade or Bowie and they certainly weren't wearing sand-coloured corduroy jackets.

The other thing about the middle Seventies was Dad getting regular work at the paper mill, which led to steak on Thursdays, school trips overseas and—within the space of a few years—we got a fridge, got the phone on and got a shower.

The amount of advice we got on how to use a fridge properly was ridiculous. Don't put eggs in, we were told, it'll make the whites go all funny. (Exactly what 'funny' looked like wasn't specified, but it wasn't a risk we were prepared to take.) Don't put butter in the door part, it'll go too hard and won't taste the same after. Keep it full: it works better if it's full. We got a chest freezer as well, which we used for the tripe and offal from the knackers yard that Dad fed to the dogs, and ice-cream that came in round metal tins that looked like surplus shells from a munitions factory.

The shower was like a gigantic stethoscope that you pushed onto the bath taps, with a showerhead at the end where you'd put the listening part onto a patient's chest. It was lethal, with either the hot or cold junction blowing out halfway through a shower, dousing you in freezing or scalding water. It didn't matter how many jubilee clips our Dad put on it, all you had to do was turn the tap a quarter notch and *bang!* it was off squirting around the bathroom. But it was still a shower and it symbolised a new and emerging cosmopolitanism in the house.

In spite of its many failings it was not the daftest gadget we got. That honour belongs to the water-powered potato peeler that Dad brought home. It was a drum-shaped affair that sat in the sink, with a hose that plugged into the cold tap. You then put potatoes in the drum part and turned on the tap at full bore, which caused the drum to spin around at a million miles an hour battering the spuds against the roughened drum wall and (theoretically at least) removing their skins. It must've drained the reservoirs of the Lake District every time we used it and the sound was like the bombardment before the first day of the Somme or one of Nelson's naval battles. After about half an hour of deafening clatter, when anyone within a kilometre radius of our house was trembling under their kitchen table with shellshock and we'd drained Windermere, some of the potatoes did indeed have some of the skins off, though most of them still had their skins on but had the texture of Henry Cooper's nose. I think it got about three or four turns before being discreetly tucked in the cupboard under the sink, where it took up room and gathered dust for a while before, one day, it wasn't there.

* * *

Sometimes as a father I'm so thoughtless, so self-absorbed, denser by far than an imploding dark star in a distant galaxy, that my teenage daughter is given cause to shout at me very loudly and very hard for a very long time. I have been known to incur her wrath through the disgusting and insensitive habit of 'looking at her' or 'breathing loudly'. As for the noises I make when I eat, well, it would strain the patience of a saint. I try to eat quietly, sometimes pressing soft lozenges of pasta against the roof of my mouth in a desperate attempt not to involve my thunderously loud, machine gun-like teeth in the action of mastication, but when I peep furtively in her direction at the dinner table I'm met with her furious dagger gaze.

I know what I must do when this happens; I know what the mature response should be. But just as Norma hooted and giggled in the doorway as I picked crankily at the wet knots on my Docs or blustered about stupid punk lyrics, so too do I find myself—against my better judgement—stifling a chuckle or a snigger as my daughter gets more and more furious, which makes me titter and snigger even more, which makes her . . . well, you get the picture.

I had the same feeling listening to a record by a punk band called Crass. The early explosion of punk splintered into all kinds of different groups, all calling themselves 'punk' but all very different. The hard, thrashy sound that lots of people associate with punk didn't emerge immediately and a lot of the early punk releases sound quite fast but they're also quite musical, just speeded up rockabilly. Really fast stuff was still associated with heavy metal; the first DJ to play The Ramones in the UK was Tommy Vance on his Friday evening heavy rock show.

But then some bright spark issued this Khmer Rouge–like Year Zero edict and within a short while it seemed like everyone was shouting into their microphones and playing everything VERY LOUDLY and VERY QUICKLY.

Crass emerged out of some squat in Essex. They got themselves black uniforms and ironic military-style graphics and made lots of records that were the LOUDEST and QUICKEST and SHOUTIEST of all. And they had stern commands printed on the sleeve, of the 'Pay no more than 45p' variety. Phwoar! I reckon The Man must have been fairly cacking His pants. It certainly seemed a bit blustery compared to the Orwellian certainty of 'Nicaragua will win'.

I had one of their LPs and I plucked it from the stack and played it, for old times' sake. Blimey. They were soooo angry, just so explosively angry about Thatcher and The Army and Nuclear Stuff and Securicor and Not Being Allowed to Sing At The Roxy that they could just about fucking well . . . fucking . . . fucking . . . AAAAARGH!!!

At which point I'm lying on the floor of my office with tear-stained cheeks worrying that I'll have a little leak if I laugh any harder.

The lead singer's name is Steve Ignorant, which is one of those names that, just seeing it, makes me giggle in the way you do when a teacher's really angry at you and you just can't help yourself. It's a name from a *Two Ronnies* parody sketch, like Jimmie Snot or Victor Crankypants.

I wrote a letter to him (Steve Ignorant, not Victor Crankypants), asking if Crass would come and play in my home town. And he wrote back! His letter's written on the back of a flyer about something worthy, knocked off while the band were in the offices of their record label, Small Wonder. I get the impression that the Crass Collective was made up of very conscientious young men and women who spent their weekends answering each and every letter they received. These days they'd have an intern tasked with the daily tweet. And Crass did indeed traipse to every corner of Britain to play to six people in some draughty hall if a teenager from that town had taken the trouble to ask them. But they must have hit the wall because Steve said, sure, we'll come and play, but you have to organise it.

The letter is signed off 'Peace & Love' with the ubiquitous circled anarchy symbol, which was a jarring contrast to the band's lyrics which often went along the lines of 'Do they owe us a living? / Course they do! Course they do! / Owe us a living? / Course they fucking do!' It was a 'moment' for me. Up till then if I'd thought of myself as anything then it'd be a punk, but I wasn't. I was just a kid who bought punk records and went to punk concerts and bought punk-related merchandise. I was everything that punk had set out to destroy.

A few of us had almost formed a band—*almost*. I'd written lyrics for three songs and maybe Mick Timpson still has them somewhere, gets them out every ten years or so and has a good old belly laugh. He was the only one of us who had a guitar and so for a few weeks we'd hitch-hike through to his house from our various scattered villages and 'rehearse'. It ended when the six-mile round trip got to be too much of a hassle; that is, as soon as the nights got cold and standing at the side of the road with my thumb out on the off chance of getting a lift to a bedroom where we'd argue about what kind of music we should play, without ever actually playing any music.

So Steve Ignorant's challenge set me back on my heels. To create or to consume: which side did I stand on? I realised that I was the perfect consumer. Is that single released with a picture sleeve? I want it. That album on coloured vinyl? That's the one for me. That 'limited edition' twelve-inch? Where do I pay?

I didn't organise the Crass gig. But I did look again at my part in the creative cycle. I started writing reviews of gigs by local punk bands and sending them in to *Sounds* and *New Musical Express* and *Smash Hits*, without ever getting a reply, let alone having one published. I didn't know exactly what it was I was doing but I was beginning to sense that what I had been doing, for all its decoration of rebellion, was just conformity.

Crass had a song called *Banned from the Roxy*. It starts 'Banned from the Roxy: OK / We never much liked playing there anyway / They said they only wanted well-behaved boys / Do they think guitars and microphones are just fucking toys?' Even at the time I thought that sounded a bit petulant but for all their angry posturing and shouty songs Crass did do something purely punk. They sat down in the back of a record shop in London and replied to a letter from a teenager in Cumbria. And opened his eyes.

* * *

From the *North Western Evening Mail*, Tuesday, 21 March 1978, 'Entertainment' page:

> *Tonight: The Harlems*
> *(Seven-piece coloured band straight from* Opportunity Knocks*)*
> *plus*
> *Black Velvet Disco*
> *Guests 50p, Members Free*
>
> *Saturday: Feminine Touch*
> *(Three gorgeous girls direct from* New Faces*)*
> *and*
> *Dougie Webb*
> *(Comedian)*

No wonder I wrote to Steve Ignorant.

* * *

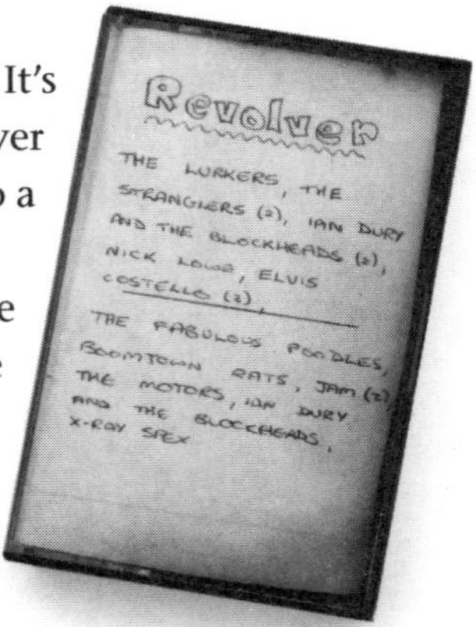

Archaeologists love this kind of thing. It's like a Roman coin found just below a layer of blackened soil that dates the trench to a precise historical event.

My version of relative dating and the Law of Superposition is this cassette tape. It's sixty minutes of recordings I've made of the TV show *Revolver*, which was a kind of ITV attempt to get on the punk bandwagon, about a year too late. The premise was that the show took place in a seedy club run by a narky, downbeat character, played by Peter Cook (who must have been down on his luck and his finances at the time) who'd opened the doors to spiky-haired louts to make a quid. As these things went it was all right, though the times (early to mid 1978) felt something like the morning after a horrible party. The Sex Pistols had imploded in the USA, The Clash didn't seem to be going anywhere, The Damned had broken up and so on.

But punk bands were still performing. The quality of the tape is terrible (because it's me holding the tiny, matchbox-sized microphone of a mono cassette recorder up to the feeble loudspeaker of our telly) but you'll hear The Lurkers, The Stranglers, Ian Dury and the Blockheads, Nick Lowe and Elvis Costello on one side, and on the other you'll hear The Fabulous Poodles, Boomtown Rats, The Jam, The Motors and X-Ray Spex.

What was on the tape before I taped over it? I can just make out, crossed out in red biro, Stevie Wonder, Queen, the Beach Boys, Rod Steward, ELO and The Who. Yes, even The Who got trashed in punk's Year Zero approach to music.

* * *

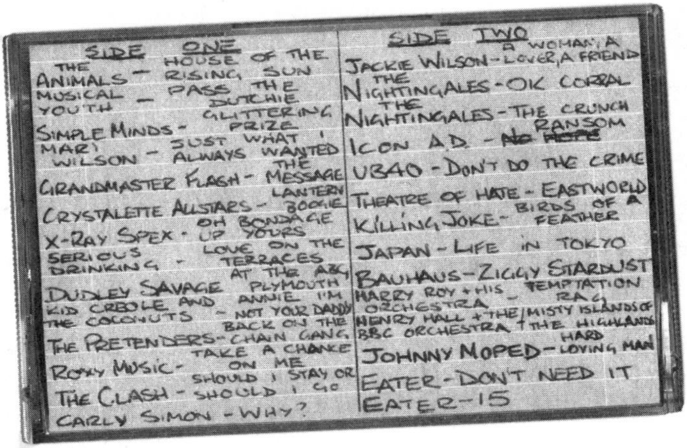

As a teenager I didn't think of myself as particularly useless. I was just doing exactly what everyone else was doing, though everyone else did seem to be doing it more successfully. At some point though, as I pulled away from my teens, I began to remember those years in a way that wasn't altogether complimentary. The poor decisions, the missed opportunities and the failure to learn from mistakes are the actions of almost every person who's ever lived but I started to look upon them as personal failures or character flaws.

Perhaps it's because in my twenties I began to mix with people who did appear to know what they were doing and where they were going. They'd been to university and were in professions, not jobs. They seemed to have gotten a head start on life that I thought I'd missed, that I'd spent fooling around in a shipyard, getting drunk, chasing girls, wasting time. It was a while before I worked out that these years were not just okay: they were, in fact, good. But by then I think I'd created this rather poor teen self-image. I'm no longer so hard on myself, and looking back at this person that I was, I've become quite fond of him. I didn't set out to reinvent myself and so this has come as quite a surprise.

A year or two after punk had burned itself out I allowed myself to like the records that I'd liked before punk and I became quite eclectic in my musical tastes. I bought lots of cheap jazz and classical music LPs; you could get decent ones for 99p from Woolworths. I'd pick them at random in the record bins, usually because I liked the cover or the name. I had no idea who anyone was; if you'd told me that Stravinsky was Bach's brother-in-law I would have accepted that without blinking. I got the Rimsky-Korsakov just because of the name; how could you not like it? For a while *Scheherazade* was my favourite LP, which is probably mega-banal for anyone who knows anything about classical music. But, prior to this, my knowledge of classical music came from Mr Kipling cake adverts.

The mix tapes were part of this period. There's lots of John Peel, he being the maverick Radio 1 DJ who broke punk and reggae and made them the musical styles of the era. Often I'd swing the dial back and forth on the stereo and stick a tape on to record before I went to the pub, then listen to see what I'd picked up when I got home. These tapes are full of diverse, colliding sounds. A bit of the Top 40 countdown interrupted by *The Organist Entertains* or Radio Luxembourg or the Shipping Forecast. I'd deliberately turn tapes over halfway through things I liked and start re-taping on the other side just for the perverse pleasure of it. I liked to have the waffle of the record announcers before and after the songs; I liked it at the time and I like it now. There's an odd bathos to these late night radio recordings that I sensed and appreciate, like the doppelganger of an overhead plane or the receding lumber of a goods train along a distant rail line.

I find in the bottom of this box an odd collection of articles I'd cut out of magazines: a review of a Dylan Thomas biography; an interview with landscape historian WG Hoskins in the *Observer*; an article on pesticide use and the decline of the large raptors in the British Isles. If I was given this stuff without knowing who it belonged to I'd describe a person with an interest in social history, politics, natural history, not the dope I'd created in my memory.

ROYAL·53
1982
ROYAL·53
1981
ROYAL·53
1980
ROYAL·53
1979

Box 5

When I first went to Australia I took a camera with me, a cheap point and press. I took quite a few photos, mostly uninspiring shots of Hyde Park Barracks or the Big Lobster at Kingston. The photos that I'd taken up until this big trip had been focused on people—jostling crowds photobombing at concerts, line-ups of reprobates at agricultural shows and unposed shots in boozers (see above)—but now I was on my own; there was rarely anyone for me to take a photo of and even less rarely anyone to take a photo of me. So lots of the shots are of the 'I was here' variety, mnemonics that would have been better served by a decent postcard (see below).

I soon worked out that they weren't any good; about three trips to the chemist to pick up envelopes of double prints and realising that a little Minolta isn't the best camera for a shot of the football action at Leichhardt Oval or the lighthouse at Byron Bay. I started not photographing and making myself commit the scene or the event to memory, as though this were somehow a superior way of storing and retrieving the occasion. I now have no memory of huge tracts of my holiday, despite commanding myself to remember them. I found a ticket stub for when I went to see a band called Killing Joke at the Chevron Club in Kings Cross. I had totally

forgotten about this until I saw the stub. It's as though it had never happened.

I read about a study in which people were split into two groups and taken around a museum. Some looked at the exhibits while others took shots with their smart phones. The smart-phone people, the study revealed, had worse recall of the items they'd been exposed to. That's a result that is likely to make us all feel a bit better and yet I'd like the researchers to come back in twenty years and see how the results pan out.

My stuff is helping me remember. They're visual triggers, setting thoughts pinballing through my mind. It's like when you see an old photo of a family gathering and find yourself focusing not on the people but on the wallpaper or the curtains, a detail you thought you'd forgotten until now.

But diaries, they're a different kettle of fish altogether.

* * *

I was talking to George. A few of us were having Friday afternoon beers at the Customs House, watching the tugboats fussing and cajoling the coal freighters in and out of the harbour. He asked me what was happening and I, only recently back from the UK holiday at the time, mentioned the packing up and imminent arrival of the five boxes. He had the great idea of a box-opening party: get a few folk around with packing knives to gut the boxes to see what spills out. Even better: we could get our kids to pull through the stuff and see what they made of it: what would a modern teen make of a slide rule, an adaptor for a seven-inch single, a postal order receipt, a flexi-single? George is a much braver, more confident and centred person than I am. He's taken risks in business and been successful. He'd host a great box-opening party.

But this was me. It was a great idea, a box-opening party, and one that was so great it caused a wave of nausea-inducing anxiety to crash over me. My stuff! People pulling it out and looking at it! Cruddy LPs and singles I could handle, schoolbooks I could cope with. But what about my diaries?

Even when the boxes arrived and (in the privacy of my own office) I opened them up, the last thing I could bring myself to look at was the batch of diaries. This is because I knew what would be in them: overly detailed records of days out to places I've forgotten about with people I haven't seen in years and most likely never will ever again; notes in angsty, crabby handwriting of rejections by girls, or of sightings of girls that I was too weak-kneed and lily-livered to approach; poorly articulated thoughts about the state of the world, the state of me, the state of my friends. Ugh!

If it weren't for the historical accident of their being stored in the cock loft for thirty years, if I'd actually dragged them around with me after leaving home that last time, I think it would be fair to say that, by now, I would have destroyed them. This seems to be the normal course of affairs with people and their diaries. As I spoke to people about the impending arrival of these boxes and what was in them, certain themes began to emerge, diary destroying being one of them.

The other theme was 'relationship to stuff'. Take the abovementioned George, for example. When George left his parents' place to go to teacher-training college they packed up his stuff, as had mine for me. It would be three years before he returned to the Monaro sheep property where he'd grown up. He went down the familiar corridor and dumped his bag in his old room. He asked his parents, 'Where's all my stuff?' They brought out the boxes of stuff that'd been in his room when he left, the things that his parents thought were important and worth keeping, the most representative things of George's youth: the school chemistry award, the best and fairest trophy, the prefect's badge, the hat-trick cricket ball. George said, 'I looked at this stuff: it was the stuff of a stranger. I asked them, "Where are my canvases and portfolios?" They said, "Your drawings? Oh, you did like your drawings, didn't you? We chucked all that out." George took a long mouthful from his schooner. Clearly, it still bit deep.

And Gina. When I talked to her about it she laughed and rolled her eyes. Gina has four kids, the youngest just finishing the HSC. She said, 'I have *everything* every one of them's ever done, ever brought home, from preschool to university. It's ridiculous but I can't not do it! The attic's absolutely bursting with the stuff, Ken thinks it's a fire hazard and he's right!' Gina, like George, had had her most valuable stuff chucked out as soon as she'd left home. The middle child of seven, space had been at a premium but, unlike George, she'd dealt with it differently.

Diaries are treated differently. Perhaps it's the small and portable nature of them, or the intensity and deeply, revealingly personal quality of what's in them, but people tend to take their diaries with them—before eventually destroying them. Alice burned hers in a 44-gallon drum in her backyard. She was new in town, in Kunanurra, her first posting, and maybe she was making a statement about her new life. Tara burnt hers without even reading them. (Burning seems to be the most common way of dealing with diaries. There's something very cleansing and cathartic and final about it.)

I'd hooked up the turntable and got a new needle, arranged the singles in alphabetical order, sifted through the schoolbooks and chucked out a fair bit of the truly redundant crap before I eventually turned a baleful eye on the small stack of diaries. I couldn't put it off any longer.

* * *

In recent years Michael Palin has published his diaries in serial form, beginning in 1969 with the birth of Monty Python and so far taking us up to 1998. They're full of entertaining anecdotes of the Pythons' working process, of meetings with famous people to discuss exciting collaborations, and of commentary on political and social upheaval. Though they're marketed as diaries I think they'd be better described as journals. The journal isn't just a record of events but is a place to expand on not-yet matured ways of thinking, to digress and ramble and allow yourself to form the philosophies and beliefs by which you'll go on to live your life. A good journal is like a school maths book with all the workings on the side of the page so that the beauty of the numbers tumbling inevitably to a clear and final answer is laid out for the reader to follow. And a good journal, such as Palin's, not only tells us about the person but evokes the time in which it was written.

The diary, in contrast, can be a very plain thing, a list of places visited, people met, items purchased. I'd expected my diaries to be a bit boring, but I was unprepared for just how mind-numbingly dull they were. If I read more than three entries at a time I started getting shooting pains through my eyes and my brain; it's like there were needles coming off the page. Even when I read about events that I have vivid memories of to this day the entry itself was cryptic or devoid of any meaningful information.

One of the key issues that makes the diaries very dull is that they're exclusively, morbidly about me, and I simply wasn't an interesting person. I hadn't worked out that not everything needs recording—even Samuel Pepys had the odd day off. If there was a blank page in the diary with a date at the top then stuff had to be written. An example from when I was working at the shipyard:

Monday, 4 October 1981
Pissed down on the way to work. Got wet through. Got an apprentice [I was a journeyman myself by this point]. It was Angela AKA Fagash Lil. Having a girl apprentice means having all these blokes hanging around. Back in the workshop Wee Archie is still giving Simon a hard time.

> *'Dae samthin ya lazy feckin twat!' he shouts for the three thousandth time, and for the three thousandth and onceth time Simon does nothing. Nightschool and it was raining so got wet again. Late home and when I got home dad have given my tea (a pie) to some bloke who knocked on the door. He was cold and wet said dad. I said I'm cold and wet! Watched* Film 82. Bladerunner. *Bring back Barry Norman. The man that does it now is rubbish.*

Did my dad really give my tea, a pie, to a tramp? It's entirely plausible. We had an open lean-to next to the house that we optimistically called 'the garage' because that's where we kept the car. In it Dad had a gas burner that he used for boiling up the tripe and sheep's heads that he fed to the dogs. Because it was open to the world anyone could use that burner, and they did. There were plenty of men wandering the roads of that corner of the world at the time. We called them 'tramps' or 'dossers', but not in a bad way. They just were. Like Roger Miller's *King of the Road*, they knew every lock that ain't locked when no one's around and I'm sure that our garage was a well-known stop on the circuit. You didn't even have to unpick the lock because there wasn't a door let alone a lock. Coming home from school, down the hill from the bus stop, on rainy winter days I'd often see steam coming out of the lean-to and, when I passed, I'd exchange shy nods with some tatty man I'd never seen before. Dad knew they came but never bothered and it's only in hindsight that I can see the generosity of spirit that was probably born from knowing what it was like to have little or nothing yourself.

I can remember Wee Archie too, a firebrand from the hard end of Glasgow, and Simon, who was a bit like me but a year two older. Simon was at the stage where he really needed to leave the warm nest of the shipyard, take a risk and plunge into the world. And Wee Archie was doing everything in his power to help him. I can hear him now, Wee Archie, berating, nagging and cajoling, and I can see Simon's placid, bovine face. They were made for each other in a crazed hellish kind of way. Maybe they're still there now, Wee Archie bent over and decrepit but still able to scream 'Dae samthin!' and Simon, balding and stooped, staring placidly back.

As for the man who was doing the cinema review show *Film 82*, I have no recollection of him. That's what Wikipedia's for. You could probably also go there to find out what was happening in the world of society and politics because you certainly weren't going to find it in my dreary diary. What was happening in politics in October 1981? Oh, just some minor event (I Googled it): the end of the hunger strikes in the Maze Prison. Obviously not worth remarking upon.

Perhaps the other division between the diary and the journal is the audience. A journal always has the potential to be read by someone other than the author; I do wonder whether, even in his nascent Python years, the ambitious and hard-working Palin had one eye on the future as he transcribed the details of his day. And I'll bet he freshened up a few dud entries; if I was going to publish my diaries as journals I'd add after *Bladerunner* 'poorly reviewed and perhaps suffering from uneven post-production but, I think, destined to become a cult classic'.

I'm not sure who I was writing my diaries for, certainly not my friends and definitely not family. The hell of the discovered diary is matched only by the nightmare of turning up to school with no clothes on. But I'm not sure that I wrote my diaries even for me. I wonder how might I have written each entry differently if I'd thought that others would read them at some point in the future.

* * *

Being a shipyard electrician is not the crazy, rock 'n' roll lifestyle that many people think it is. Between the drugs and

PACIFIST / DIRECT ACTION

The questionaire was put together under the name of a pacifist direct action group. Its been done to find out how many people hold similar radical views to the ones expressed in this leaflet with the aim of setting up a communication network between people who want to change things and do something about it.

We are people who agree with one or more of the following ideals

NUCLEAR DISARMAMENT
FEMINISM (women who choose to lead their own lives, who are independant of sexual stereotypes and believe that they have an important role in life other than the conventional wife/mother/childbearer.)
Prevention of cruelty to children/women
GAY LIBERATION (for women and men, the freedom to choose ones own sexuality regardless of whether the relationship is woman/woman or man/man)
ANTI-TERRORIST
A NON-RACIST SOCIETY
ANARCHISM (people free from the domination of one person over another)
INDIVIDUALISM
ANIMAL LIBERATION (prevention of nastyness to animals, especially experiments on them)
ECOLOGY (Friends of the Earth)
Anti-uniforms, government organisations e.g. schools, public industries as they stand.
Control of how resources are used by everyone that is affected by them.
ABOLITION OF THE WORK ETHIC
No fox hunting
No leaders, No followers

---

1) Are you involved with any people who have similar views to the above - ____________
2) Do you want to meet people who hold those views/or some of those views ____________
3) Are you prepared to do something (e.g. come on demonstrations or organise gigs.)
4) Do you feel you have the freedom to make decisions for yourself ____________
5) If not, how have you been prevented ____________
6) Of the ideals we put forward which do you agree/sympathise with ____________
7) How far do you agree with the views and what are your interpretations of them ____________

Please write and tell us

SYMBOLS
54a WOOD STREET,
MARYPORT
CUMBRIA

groupies there are alternators that need re-winding, terminals that have to be crimped and things that need to be connected up to other things. So that we could learn all about this more responsible side of our trades we went off to the local tech for night school and block release.

We did subjects with names like 'Utilisation'. The mere mention of the name is enough to make me feel instantly torpid; my legs and arms take on three times their normal mass, my eyelids feel like veils of heavy uncooked dough and my breathing slows to the rate of a hibernating bear. There were other subjects with names like 'Installation', 'Applications: Heavy' and 'Applications: Light'. What were they about? I've got no idea. I can vaguely remember that in one of them we had to work out how many lightning conductors would be needed on a church with X number of spires of Y height, and in another we had to work out the volume of air moving through a warehouse with a roller door (dimensions provided) at one end and two ordinary doors (dimensions provided) at the other, the roller door being opened A times per hour and the ordinary doors B times. There are formulas for this kind of thing so that you can work out how big the air conditioning unit needs to be for such a warehouse. Believe me. The classrooms at tech were old, painted in the smear-proof cream, burgundy and racing green popular in austerity Britain and still used by the vat-load in the area's schools.

I'd been up to Carlisle to see Crass, the Very Angry But Conscientious People I mentioned earlier. On this occasion they were very angry about Greenham Common air base which, to be fair, a lot of folk were pretty cranky about at the time. It was a benefit gig to raise money for bolt cutters so that the Greenham women could break in and wreak havoc in a peaceful, non-violent way. Of course the gig was crawling with fellow travellers handing out leaflets on everything from animal liberation to the emerging police state to the perils of nylon underpants. It was a grand night and I accumulated quite a batch of these leaflets because it was a great way to meet the lovely young lasses who were handing them out. There's a girl's name and phone number on the back of the flyer from Maryport Pacifist / Direct Action group, the one that promotes FEMINISM (in all caps) and believes that women 'have an important role in life other than the conventional wife / mother / childbearer'.

So I'm sitting in Utilisation doing the 1981 equivalent of updating my Facebook status on my smart phone; that is, leafing through these leaflets, with all their ironically militaristic slogans and logos and typefaces. And the man who was running the lesson, a guy called Fred Bell, must have caught me. My diary entry reads:

> *Friday, 23 October 1981. Fred caught me looking at the Crass handouts and started droning on about 'When I was in Berlin before the war . . .' Zzzzz.*

I'm finding it hard to type at the moment because my fingers have curled into fists of rage and fury and shame. Remember what I said about The Airfix Gang a while back?

I know—I *know*—that however stupid, immature and facile that I was at the time, I wasn't *that* stupid, immature or facile. I mean, I read the Big Papers! And I know that I would have listened to what Fred had to say, even if I did so while affecting a posture of sneering insouciance—whatever that looks like. So why did I describe him as 'droning on' and why oh why did I end the entry with that infantile 'Zzzzz'? What a twat.

* * *

When she was about nine years old my daughter put the gifts for the family that she'd made or bought at the school fete under the tree. I couldn't figure out what mine was based on its shape, and didn't try to spoil things by squeezing it, shaking it

CRASS

pic: Pete Gilbert.

It was a Sunday afternoon and curiosity had led us to this farm labourers cottage in the Essex countryside. Concealed well off the beaten track we had managed to trace down a band that had sent our imaginations spinning when we first saw them supporting Cuddly Toys at the Moonlight in West Hampstead. Their name is Crass and their dress is black, they are vegetarian and their music/noises are fast, short, angry statements against what they feel is wrong in the world. All appear to be very serious in their belief but whether you believe what they say is another matter? We've just written our questions and objections together with their answers and explanations. And the rest is up to you? We began by asking the inevitable question, who's idea was it to form Crass? Steve: "I came to live here and I told Penny that I was thinking of starting a band, and that I would like to sing. Penny had a set of drums and offered to drum for me. Then all the members joined as they passed through the house, it just sort of grew like that." But why was the band formed? Steve: "Well, for a start, I went to see the Clash in Bristol and Joe Strummer was up there saying "Go out and do it", so I thought 'I will' and I just felt that I just wanted to say something and do something, y'know, make my own stand. But I think we've all got different reasons for joining the band." But how did you come to live here and how did you find this place? Steve: "Well, I just met everybody here." G: "It's been established for about 12 years now and people just come and go all the time - there's been a band here before and the whole house has always worked along these lines. There has always been a facility here for people to do what they want to do. Whether they use it or not is another matter." Tell us something about the household, is it a family? G: "No, not really, basically it just works on respect, mutual respect. Everyone here is an individual and we just happen to have very similar views - but it's coming in a lot of different directions - that's why it's got a lot of energy and power. Nobody's trying to dictate or anything." At this stage a large brown tea-pot appears on the scene and after we've all been asked whether we take sugar etc, we asked how they would describe themselves? Would they describe themselves as anarchist's?

ANARCHY

G: "Well, you'd have to define how you're using the term really - Pacifist's - Anarchist's maybe. Well we're anarchist's in thought but I don't think any of us, at the moment, intend to pick up a gun and start firing But there are several forms of anarchy? Phil: "No there isn't! Anarchy is just what it means, without state...." G: "It means complete chaos" Pete: "In the dictionary it means a state without government...." Andy: "The thing is, we're talking about ourselves and our relationship with other people. But when you start trying to classify us, well that's exactly what we're trying to get away from. Once we get labeled with whatever, well that's what we're against! We are people and we're trying to relate to other people as people, and we're trying to get them to see themselves as people, rather than as part of a mass. I mean, I suppose a lot of the things we do could be classified as anarchic, but we are people." Phil then goes on to explain even further: "A simple example is the unemployed in this country, I mean economically it's no crime to be unemployed. What is the crime, is to not mind being unemployed because you've got better things to do. It's no crime to actually lead your own life the way you want to, as long as you're not affecting other people. The real crime is, when it points out the rest of what is going on." We challenged them at this point by stating that not everyone thought about things as deeply as they do? What about the ordinary person and guessing. On the big day she proudly presented it to me. I unwrapped it: it was a clipboard. I think I managed to stammer something along that lines of 'Just what I always wanted!' She replied, 'I wanted to get you a clipboard because you always shout at us when we take your other one.' My mouth moved like that of a goldfish for a few seconds but no sound came out. What in God's name was she on about? Thankfully it was Christmas morning and we quickly moved on to the Terry's chocolate oranges and other pre-breakfast rituals, but I had to come back to her later in the day and ask her: (a) Do I really shout at you when you borrow my other clipboard?; and (b) What other clipboard?

I never did get to the bottom of it, but it was a window into her perception of the world, and of my place in it. It seems that in her mind I was some fierce stationery ogre, greedily defending the family's hoard of protractors and highlight pens from the meddling hands of small children.

Even if she doesn't mention it anymore there's a good chance that deep in her neurological pathways there's a link between father, clipboards and male aggression. 'And no matter how many clipboards we bought for my old dad,' she'll chuckle to the wide-eyed grandchild on her knee, 'there were never enough! Oh, he was a real one for the clipboards was your old granddad!'

And I know that I'm doing the same thing with my own parents. At least in that previous diary entry I actually mention my Dad. I was nineteen and still living at home and my parents were still large presences in my life, but you wouldn't think so from the diary entries. They're more like shadows on the cave wall of Plato's *Republic* or extras in a movie, occasionally pulling into focus but only to further the central theme of Me.

There are lots of descriptions of nights out and records bought and people hooked up with. There's a decent-sized subsection covering the various bits of my bike to have fallen off or in need of repair; I must have spent a third of my life on the concrete of the garage floor filing points, tightening chains and tracing electrical faults in the wiring harness. No emotional insight. No paragraph beginning, 'Today I'm feeling . . .' No sense of what I felt or thought about anything.

I had the ability to describe events but it seems that I didn't have the ability to put feelings down in words. Things were 'excellent!' or they were 'rubbish'. When I'd done something stupid or been rebuffed or dumped I don't write about it, other than in a kind of coy meta-language that covers up my emotions and inner feelings. There's no bewildered 'How could she?' or 'Why would he say that?' Just lines like this following a dumping: 'Flat. Might give Friday a miss.'

One entry says, 'After dad went to bed me and mam talked for ages without any cross words.' It's tantalisingly cryptic. I don't remember it at all and I wish I'd just added something such as 'talked for ages about life' / 'her fears for her declining health' / 'her ambitions for dot dot dot' / 'her sense that her life has been wasted and what she really wanted to do was blah'. Seeing the entry and having no memory of it is almost worse than just having no memory of it at all.

* * *

All this trying to be in the world, this growing, this reaching out that occasionally pokes its head up in the diaries. It's everything that I no longer am.

I was recently at the funeral of a friend's mother, the second funeral in as many weeks. A lovely, reserved service with the grandchildren of the deceased playing a beautiful and moving musical recital. This was a nice people's funeral and so it was quite classy, with delicious finger food served on special plates that looked a bit like an artist's palette, with a depression to stop your cup sliding around and room for a spring roll and a cupcake. At the do after Norma's funeral it was a bit more boisterous; I remember at the end nearly dying laughing at my Uncle Donald, who's well into his eighties but still likes a drink or six, when he showed me how to wrestle a broom.

Things at this funeral were more genteel. Phoebe and I have kids about the same age and we were talking about wisdom, comparing ourselves to our own kids, who seem so much more emotionally mature than we were at the same age. She said that she felt like she'd been gaining wisdom throughout her thirties and forties but then this accumulation just seemed to just stop—almost flatline—after fifty and that there was no more gaining of wisdom.

I know what she means, although thinking about it I feel that although I'm not getting any wiser I do feel that my centre of gravity is lower or closer to the earth, my core is more stable. I'm not sure that this in itself makes me any wiser but I do feel that it makes me less inclined to be buffeted by the opinions of others.

I haven't kept a diary for years and I wonder whether it's just because I got too busy or because I was no longer trying to work out who I was or what I thought about things.

* * *

When my sister left home for teachers' college she took her possessions in a big trunk. She has it still, its metal corners bashed and dinged from a thousand journeys from upstairs flats to share houses to restoration homes. She took her world with her; I left mine behind. It says a lot about us and about our way of viewing the world and our future place in it. I read her decision as reflecting her certainty about what lay ahead and mine as reflecting my ambivalence. I left my stuff for thirty years, never once showing an interest in coming back to get it. If it hadn't been for a government scheme to put insulation in my dad's attic it'd be there still. And yet the not getting rid of it says something too, and I'm guessing it's about my unwillingness to fully commit to a future in Australia when I headed out here, and to let go of a past in England.

We both left home, my sister and me. And yet now, after forty years of living in various towns and cities, my sister is living within a few miles of where she began. She's taken up the allotment next to Dad's house that he gave up a couple of years back when the rollies caught up with his lungs and he found it almost impossible to push a shopping trolley around the supermarket, never mind turn over a quarter acre of potatoes.

Of the reasons for leaving the village—the many, many reasons for leaving—I think that the most resonant is articulated by Lorna Sage, a feminist academic brought up in rural Shropshire. Sage fell pregnant at fifteen but persevered through sheer determination and personal brilliance to become a leading authority on women writers. She describes village life as 'the peculiar hell of having to live with such substantial ghosts from your past'. It's a quote that, as soon as I read it, I felt compelled to copy into my notebook.

I vividly remember dragging myself out of my bedroom (I'd have been seventeen or eighteen) one Saturday morning, bleary-eyed and hung-over, and bumping into Norma in the kitchen. She had a knowing look on her face, and said, 'Big night last night, eh?' And the cold chill that ran from my scalp, down my spine and the backs of my legs to the soles of my feet as I tried to remember what we'd done. Drink. Pubs. A flashback of going into the old-time dance that the pensioners ran in the Band Hall every second Friday. It was probably all very innocent in the grand scheme of things, but everything that happened on a Friday was relayed, replayed and analysed at the front counter of the Co-op on a Saturday morning.

Hilary Clinton popularised the phrase 'it takes a village to raise a child' a while back. I suppose it's true. Learning to do certain things under the supervision of the network of relatives and friends who all have a direct line of communication to your parents means that there's always a guiding hand or stern voice to curb the excesses of childhood. So the village raises the child, but then the child becomes the teenager. The network becomes a web. The mentor becomes a drag anchor. The child begins to despise the village.

Leaving seemed like the only option. It wasn't; I've got plenty of friends who stayed and have led perfectly contented lives. But in my mind it had to happen. I felt that too many people thought they knew me better than I knew myself. It's common amongst teenagers to believe this because teenagers seriously believe that everyone else is thinking about them and talking about them all the time. It seems laughable now, from the lofty heights of my fifties, but kids can't be told.

* * *

I record in my diary that a bunch of us thumbed it through to a dance at a nearby town. There was a disco in the Victory Hall preceded by a live act, a local heavy metal band called Bitches Sin. Though it may have been Bitch's Sin. Or even Bitches' Sin. I never thought to ask, and now I might never know.

* * *

As well as all the usual stuff about people and events, I had a habit of recording the microscopically dull details of my life. An example of this is the eating of hot chips.

> *Friday, 31 August 1979. Had chips and went home.*
> *Thursday, 19 March 1981. Chip shop closed.*
> *Saturday, 21 June 1980. Had chips.*

The references to the eating of chips are the heavy metronome of my life: *tock!* had chips; *tock!* chip shop closed; *tock!* had chips and went home. It makes me want to clasp my hands to my cheeks and do a Munchian scream face. *Nooooo!* Maybe if I'd recorded the quality of the chips it might have been a fraction more interesting but I don't even do that. 'Had chips. Their crispy, crunchy texture indicates that they'd been double fried, possibly in goose fat.' 'Decided not to have salt, as this may impact upon my blood pressure in future decades.' 'Disappointing chips. Think they've changed their potato variety to King Edwards; a false economy in my opinion.'

Once again, it's the absence that's intriguing. Did I write about chips because I didn't have them very much and so, when I did, it was worth recording? I don't think so. Even now my eating habits are pretty ordinary, and in our house a full English breakfast dripping with animal fat is referred to as a 'Cumbrian salad'.

Maybe it was because I was buying takeaway food, which still seemed like a treat. If for some reason I had to go into town with Mam on a Saturday, a trial that must have been as annoying for her as it was for me, the grand treat before we got the train home was a malted coffee at Bruccianni's coffee lounge in the main street. Along with fish and chips or a hot dog at the dog races, this was the extent of my takeaway food eating.

So maybe I was just excited at having some disposable income and the opportunity to spend it how I liked. It's an optimistic interpretation that I'm going to console myself with.

* * *

I'm in a reading group and every year we pick a classic, modern or olden time, and once we did *The Catcher in the Rye*. This was a great experience for me but not for Antoinette, who had considered it to be her favourite book of all time but didn't like it at all upon re-reading it.

For me it not only stood the test of time but actually got better. On first reading I probably empathised with Holden Caulfield; I honestly can't remember if I did so but it's the kind of predictable thing I would have done. And then came my adult reading in which, of course, Holden is the type of slack-jawed mouth breather who, these days, would be chewing up his parents' broadband allowance watching *Jackass* videos on YouTube and throwing up moronic Instagram posts. The goddam phoney. In the re-reading the adults leapt off the pages, a small army of people trying to offer guidance and support and steer young Holden into something approaching a right direction. But of course he was too up himself and stupid and self-absorbed and . . . such a goddam *teenager* to notice.

There was a time when I was an adult in Australia and my grown-up Australian friends and I didn't think or talk about kids. Then someone got pregnant and someone else got pregnant and then The Wife and I got pregnant and then somehow everywhere I looked there were kids. Sometimes the kids were friends' kids and sometimes the friends only became friends because they were the parents of my own kids' friends. When you've got kids their progress and development and hilarious things they've done and said can fill any conversational vacuum, or the Internet, or both. I wonder if my parents talked about me and my sister in the same way? Did they agonise over every subject choice at school or activity as much as I seem to do with mine?

In my diaries my parents are *there* but they're not there. They appear in mercurial ways and it's only on rare occasions that they seem to have any agency in my life, other than the edict to 'get a trade behind you' when leaving school. This is the Holden Caulfield view. I wonder now: did they worry about me? Perhaps they only insisted that I go and get a trade because, knowing me better than I did myself, they realised that if I went to further education I'd waste a good ten years of my life stumbling around in yellow dungarees trying to find out what it was that I wanted to do. If I got a job though I'd be forced to learn the rules of getting up in the morning and going to a place where I had commitments and there were expectations of me; then I might make a half-decent human being.

For a while in my twenties I was cranky at them for this and saw the apprenticeship and the years of working in a job I didn't much want as having been wasted. I was still very much a teenager until I was twenty-five and so, like all teenagers, I externalised all the bad things. It's always someone else's fault. They made me do it. If it wasn't for them I'd be . . . With the tiny skerrick of maturity that came with growing up I began to take some responsibility for my actions—or, more often and more accurately, lack of actions. Later than many people, it dawned on me that the world wasn't hanging around twiddling its thumbs waiting for me to be ready. It was just spinning around the sun, year after year, and if I wasn't ready well, hey, there's plenty who are.

Perhaps like Holden Caulfield I had mentors offering me advice and direction but, like Holden Caulfield, I was too self-absorbed to acknowledge them. He wasn't what you'd call a mentor in the classic sense of the word but I remember Wee Archie having a crack at me after I'd moaned about the yard one day: 'Don't like what you're doing here? Well fuck off. It's as simple as that.' It was, which was the scary thing, and which is why it took me so long to realise that what happened next in my life was entirely up to me.

* * *

The other week I was cycling home from the pub with Tom after quiz night. We've fallen into the comfortable relationship of two elderly buffers who can have the same conversation on a regular basis without noticing, or indeed caring when we do in fact notice. Sometimes one of our friends will point out to us the endless loop of our conversation, but rather than feeling bad about this state of affairs it's like greeting an old pal you haven't seen in a while: Which was the best in the Aurora toy series, the Chamber of Horrors or the glow-in-the-dark Wolfman? And was it Wolfman or the Werewolf? Would David Bowie's latest LP ever have been released if he was new on the scene? Is the English slang name for your old feller pronounced 'tadger' or 'todger'?

One of the recurring tropes is this: 'Is it different to be young now compared to previous ages?' Tom thinks it is: the Internet has changed everything irrevocably. Not only can kids access unthinkable amounts of data and information, there is also unthinkable amounts of data and information stored about them. Things that happened in the past and disappeared into the mythology of pub tales are now Snap-chatted and Instagrammed for the whole world to laugh at, share and re-tweet. It's created people differently: Mick Jagger could only have existed in our time.

Me, I think it isn't all that different. The Internet has certainly made more stuff available, but in many ways it's just more stuff. Technologies come and go, from the printing press to the telegram, but people's needs and desires remain resolutely, stubbornly the same. A girl's life can be ruined if someone with a smart-phone takes a compromising picture of her with a young man at a rock concert but these are the exceptions rather than the rules of most people's lives; anyway, it's what drove her and the young man into one another's arms that's the real show in town.

There's a subset to this conversation that usually involves our children, who are now at the age where they're leaving or have left school and are getting about in the world. We do that unfavourable comparison thing that (and I shudder to hear myself even think it in my head) begins, 'When I was his/her age . . .' Tom's daughter is carving out a career in fashion and, for her nineteenth birthday, I gave her a 1981 edition of *iD* magazine,

which I pulled from the depths of Box 5. I remember buying it in London; the date's easy to remember because it was my twentieth birthday and a gang of us had got the train down there to have a weekend in the big smoke. It was remarkable how contemporary some of the fashions and poses were in this magazine even though it was over thirty years old. It'd be like me in 1981 looking at a fashion magazine from 1949. (I haven't got a picture of the cover of *iD* because it's Charlotte's now; instead, I've put a selection of the many, many other music and fashion magazines that I wasted my money on as well.)

In our family we've somehow contrived to get four mobile phones, a landline and an Internet connection on our phone bill. I've got an app on my phone that tells me how much data I've used each month and, because mine's the name on the invoices, I get to see what everyone else in the family's used too. The kids inevitably burn up their allowance faster than Telstra can boil up a new batch of interweb. My daughter's got a bit of a handle on it but my son? Well . . .

One month he'd managed to smash his data allowance and had run up a monster bill. Again. Repayment usually takes the form of gardening, car washing and ploughing through baskets of ironing while I *pfft* in the background and moan about what I was doing at his age. I try not to be the Yorkshireman who lived in a cardboard box on the M6 but, damn it, it's hard. After all, I *was* riding my motorbike for miles and miles through wind and sleet to work forty hours in a submarine.

The particular month that my son blew his bill again he was seventeen years and seven months old; I was that exact age in July 1979. I went back and looked at my diary for that month, which was quite momentous as I was about to leave the shelter of the apprentice training school, have my first shipyard fortnight and then, in August, I'd be out and into the yard proper. But most of the entries were about going to see bands, buying records, going out and getting refused service in pubs or getting served in pubs and . . . Ugh.

I tried one more time, just for the sake of it. I worked out how old I was when my dad was the age I am now and picked out the date: my nineteenth birthday. It made depressing reading. I'd got my marks back from two exams in my electrical engineering course, both of which I'd failed, and then I got a flat front tyre on the way home from night school.

It was at this point that I knew I had to do what everyone does: burn the lot of them. There was no value in keeping them. I could learn nothing about myself or about my son or about how I might have behaved in his situation or he in mine. It's time to get rid of the lot. Only Michael Palin hangs on to his diaries forever.

* * *

Every electrical cable installed on a submarine or surface vessel has to be tested to ensure there are no breaks or abrasions in the insulation. You don't want to get to the bottom of the Bay of Biscay or under the polar icecaps to find out that the cable powering your engines has a nasty nick in it.

To do this the cables are dunked into vats of water with their ends sticking out of glands in the lid of the vat. This lid is then closed and bolted tight shut and then the water is pressurised using a huge, noisy old compressor. A machine then sends an electrical signal through the wire and checks that there are no short circuits that would indicate some failure in the insulation.

This was my job for a while, back in the shipyard. It was great: just me in this darkened shed with rows of pressurised vats. Once the cables were in and the pressure was up there was not much else to do, except to read the gauges every hour or so. I got loads of book reading done, mostly from my sister's prescribed reading list or books pulled at random from the shelves of the town library.

It was a perfect environment in which to read the classics: quiet and undisturbed—apart from the occasional angry *drrrrrr!* of a compressor. You could really lose yourself in a book. I remember reading *The Power and the Glory* and, at my shift's end, literally staggering when I re-entered the daylight of the afternoon sun outside the compressor shed. My head was still with the whisky priest in the Mexican villages. Its impact on me was profound. Here's how I described the moment in my diary:

> *Friday, 21 August 1981. Reading a book by Graham Greene,* Power and the Glory. *It's depressing.*

Here are some other gems that show just how quickly my powers of criticism were developing:

> *Monday, 12 May 1980.* Catch 22. *A bit odd but quite good.*
> *Saturday, 19 July 1980. Me and Karen were going to see the* Rocky Horror Picture Show *but that fell through, so we went to see* Apocalypse Now *which was excellent.*

Does it sound like I'm becoming a little discerning? Nah. If *Apocalypse now* was 'excellent' then measure it against this:

> *Saturday, 17 May 1980. Watched* Champion the Wonder Horse, *which was excellent.*

My film reviews often contained dense levels of meta-criticism within a succinct, almost terse, review:

> *Friday, 27 January 1978. Went to see* One Flew Over the Cuckoo's Nest *at the Roxy. It was a good film but had a depressing ending.*

No shit? But wait, it gets better:

> *Wednesday, 31 May 1978. Went to see* The Stud *– X!!! Not bad, but not much story to it.*

Not much of a story to it? What did I think I was going to see—*Annie Hall*? Was I sixteen or ninety-six?

* * *

For Christmas holidays this year the family spent a week in northern Victoria. A friend inherited a tiny fibro shack that her father and his friends used when they went trout fishing in the Sixties and we all pile in there, three or four families squeezed into bunks and in tents and in the tiny caravan that sits on blocks out the back. It's grand 'one in, all in' fun but it does have its down side: you sleep when the last person goes to bed (usually when the last bottle of grog's been drained) and wake when the first person rises (when the kids start rustling through the kitchen). So this year The Wife did a bit of Googling and found a place on a beef cattle farm a couple of kilometres away.

It was perfect: self-contained and air-conditioned. We got to know the owners of the farm, a lovely couple who were seventh-generation residents of the valley. 'I'll take you up the back and show you the old cabin,' said Angus, the owner, one day when he dropped round with some sausages he'd made himself from a killer he'd dropped a couple of weeks back. 'It's got a bit of history in it. You'd be interested.'

We went up in his LandCruiser, about a half-hour's drive up winding tracks and past cleared fields full of lazing bullocks with their trusting, quizzical eyes. The cabin itself wasn't what we expected; it wasn't some battler shack from the olden days but was new; in fact, it was Angus who'd built it. And he'd built it for a specific purpose.

Its outside walls were studded with obsolete tools and agricultural machinery parts and Angus delighted in asking us 'What do you think that's for?' and laughing at our modern, citified attempts to work out what function some rusty-bladed old piece of pressed metal might have been used for. It was not unlike a thousand country pubs in that sense, but the inside was different, very different. Here, Angus had stored and displayed seven generations' worth of his family's goods and belongings. There were top hats and looking glasses, embroidered quilts and shipping manifests, muskets and leather boots, photographs of bullock teams and men with axes next to the stumps of felled giants, glass cabinets with trinkets and medicine bottles, shelves with Bibles and letters home from the Western Front. It was fascinating and breathtaking and, as Angus showed us each item and the story behind it and traced its provenance back to one ancestor or another, it became deeply oppressive. I asked him whether he'd recorded any of this detail, and I asked about his children. Angus brusquely mentioned a son, a diesel mechanic working in the mines over in Western Australia who didn't have much of an interest in this kind of thing, and I felt the immense weight of those seven generations bearing down up his shoulders. To maintain a shrine is to take on a huge responsibility.

I look around my writing desk, my office. I don't want to be remembered as this person, with all this tack and nonsense. Here are some things that are in my possession, and about which I know nothing. A button from a South African Heavy Artillery uniform. A bottle opener from the Johannesburg Brewery. A silver scallop-shaped spoon, sole survivor of a once large service. Some things I know a little about:

the silver teapot that was presented to my great-grandparents on the occasion of their silver wedding anniversary by their Methodist church group. The buttons and brooch mounted on a piece of card with the words 'Best girl in school' that was presented in 1911 to Nanna Sally by her headmaster. The side plate with the Chinese motif, last of those brought back by my Uncle Malcolm after one of his Merchant Navy stints in the East.

The stuff around me tells a partial, indiscriminate story. I feel like a gigantic whale shark, one of those behemoths of the deep that glide silently through the ocean with the massive gape of their mouth permanently open, allowing books and badges and brochures and beermats and records to tumble in without judgement or prejudice.

* * *

I'm reading a series of Facebook posts that lay out in gory detail the unhappy saga of Dennis, a friend who is emptying his parents' house following their deaths, within three months of one another. Obviously he's deeply saddened but what's making the process particularly unpleasant is that his brother—who distanced himself from Dennis and their parents while they were alive—has accused Dennis of theft and fraud and stealing his inheritance. It's got to the point where an apprehended violence order has been invoked and, the last time Dennis visited the house to empty it of his parents' belongings for charity shops, he had to be accompanied by a policeman.

Another friend has not spoken to her sister for four years; since their mother died, in fact. Again, it was left to one sibling to see to the sale of the family home and its contents, and again it was a fraught affair with accusations and counter-accusations. Anna's sister accused her of squirrelling away the best of the heirlooms, of somehow contriving to have the house valued in such a way that it benefitted Anna more than her sister. But what was, if you'll pardon the expression, the final nail in the coffin of their relationship was the disposal of their mother's ashes. In spite of several calls and emails the younger sibling showed no interest in being a part of their disposal or interment. Anna thinks that her sister should be involved and that they should do this together, even if it's the last thing that they ever do together. Anna is sad and angry and can't bring herself to dispose of the ashes by herself, without her sibling; they've become too symbolic of their failed relationship. It seems that even after our deaths our stuff, our very ashes, can represent us and our relationships in ways we can't imagine while we're alive.

* * *

Carl and Esther have a beautiful property up in the Hunter Valley. It's always a treat to go there because they are the perfect hosts: artists with an eye for detail. The place has a rustic charm that, on closer examination, reveals the hard work that's gone into making it look entirely natural. In winter we light a fire and in summer we drink beer and occasionally jump into the brown water of the dam to cool off.

We were lounging around on one such hot day and got onto this subject: is there a word for the nostalgia you feel for something that didn't actually happen? We'd arrived at this point after some circular rambling about recent TV shows by Kevin McCloud (in which he built a tiny house out of leftovers) and Hugh Fearnley-Whittingstall (who seems able to do everything from whipping up a rustic feast by foraging in the hedgerows, to making a set of bagpipes from a willow stick and a pig's bladder). Whenever I see McCloud's tiny-house building or Fearnley-Whittingstall's summery gatherings where everyone's eating seaweed and acorn fritters I think, 'Yeah, that'd be me, if I still lived in England. I'd be hanging out with those guys and doing that.' And I feel a kind of warm nostalgia for this thing that never happened, and never will.

It's how I feel with this stuff.

* * *

Every time we come back from a holiday visiting my dad in the UK the kids comment for weeks afterwards how their T-shirts or pyjamas 'smell of England': a mixture of English washing powder, Golden Virginia tobacco, spray-on furniture polish and wallpaper paste. But eventually, after a few runs through the front-loader, the smell fades away.

It's now summer in Australia. The boxes are losing their English attic mustiness. Some of the LP sleeves are falling apart where the glue that's held them together for thirty years is dried out and crumbling. I open a scrapbook and hold the thick cardboard pages close to my face and inhale; it's still there, in the paper fibres, but most of the objects are now almost completely odourless.

* * *

When this book was getting close to being finished I asked the artist Trevor Dickinson to draw some of the items from the boxes, with the idea that they might be chapter openings.

Trevor and I were born within a month of one another, were both raised in regional England and share many cultural markers and landmark memories. I gave him a batch of Norma's seven-inch singles to draw—the dreaded Richard Harris, The Supremes, The Hollies and so on—and we were talking about how fragile they seemed, their paper sleeves worn thinner than Bible pages. He picked up *Downtown* by Petula Clark, the song that's playing in my memory of watching Norma get ready for a Friday night out, filling the bathroom with a haze of hairspray, and he says, 'This is the first record I ever remember hearing. I've got this vivid memory of being behind the bars of a playpen and watching my mum doing the hoovering and *Downtown*'s on the radio. And what's really weird is that I was watching *Never Mind the Buzzcocks* and that English comedian, what's his name, Phil Jupitus, he said that *Downtown* is the first record he ever remembers hearing.' And I'm struck dumb. Is my memory of standing at the end of the hallway watching Norma get ready for a night out as *Downtown* plays on the Dansette even a memory at all? Or is it the case that if you take a whole lot of kids born at roughly the same time and feed them on a diet of the same cultural landmarks for fifty years they'll all somehow end up with the same soundtrack to their childhood?

I asked myself at the beginning whether seeing this stuff would change my memory or my opinion of myself in any way. It did. My memory of myself was not very complimentary: a gormless kid bobbing like a cork on the tide of life steered by the wind and the elements. I've been reminded that the reality was different. I was more motivated than I give myself credit for. I had a sense of dissatisfaction, one that propelled me to different places and new challenges throughout my life. I didn't recognise at the time that I had mentors but I did have people who invested in me, whether it was my sister and her reading lists or Wee Archie's reminders that taking control of my life was as easy as saying, 'I'm going to do it.' And then having the gumption to do it.

* * *

'A happy man has no past, while an unhappy man has nothing else.' That's Richard Flanagan, in his novel *The Narrow Road to the Deep North*, paraphrasing Dostoyevsky and a thousand other pocket philosophers before and since. I'm not an unhappy man by any stretch, though I am prone to being glum and morose. I'm still that kid who got off on reading Kafka and Wodehouse back to back.

I'm thankful that I haven't become unhappy by revisiting my past. The past can be deeply disappointing when you see it close up—the best man's speech that had everyone in stitches will barely cause the flicker of a smile when you see the video a few years later—but seeing this past, much of which I'd forgotten about or blanked out, has been quite comforting.

* * *

'Anything [that is] unfinished when I die is to be burnt.' This is Patrick White in a letter to the National Library of Australia. Franz Kafka, in a letter to his friend and literary executor Max Brod, said, 'Dearest Max, my final request. Everything I leave behind in the way of diaries, manuscripts, letters, from others and my own, sketches, and so forth, to be burned completely and unread.'

Yeah, right. The bits and pieces of one of White's works in progress were published after his death as *The Hanging Garden*. The manuscript was about a third of what White had mapped out before abandoning it and I'm sure he'd be massively pissed off to know that his agent had got him a killer deal with Random House. And if Max Brod had been a real friend to Kafka then we wouldn't have *The Trial* or *The Castle* or *Amerika*.

Ted Hughes has been dogged throughout his life by his relationship with Sylvia Plath. The fact the she became something of a feminist icon and inspired volumes and volumes of literary analysis drove Hughes to seek more privacy and distance which, of course, only fuelled the public's desire to intrude even further. As Janet Malcolm wrote, in her book about Hughes and Plath, 'After we are dead, the pretence that we may somehow be protected against the world's careless malice is abandoned.'

The world's careless malice.

We spend so much of our lives trying to leave our mark—a book, a painting, two vast and trunkless legs of stone in a desert. The 'destroy all my papers' edict is part of the desire to control the image of yourself that those left behind will bear for the generation or so until you're forgotten. But it's a half-hearted command, one delivered with a complicit wink. And anyway, who cares? People will 'make' you with the bits they've got, or haven't got, and if they haven't got anything they'll make it up. Janet Malcolm again: 'as everyone knows who has ever heard a piece of gossip, we do not "own" the facts of our lives at all. This ownership passes out of our hands at birth, at the moment we are first observed.'

Once again I look around my office, crowded with this stuff from the past. Is this how I remember myself, or how I want to be remembered by others?

I know the answer. Don't ask someone to burn it for you. Burn it now.

A HOUSE FULL OF STUFF

I'm home again, the England home. It's the middle of the night, I'm lying in bed and I'm thinking about this oblong house and how I'd renovate it if it was mine. Maybe I'd knock out that wall between the bathroom and the back bedroom and make it into one big, luxurious bathroom with an Australian-strength shower that actually gets you wet all over. Maybe demolish the brick sheds that obscure the view of the Lake District hills and put in a conservatory. And, of course, the loft. There's always, the loft.

My thoughts are broken by the Westminster chime of a doorbell. It's not someone at the door I'm hearing but the sound of the button-operated alarm we've rigged up next to Dad's bed. I drag myself out of my bed and pull on a warm top, stub my toe. The clock flashes 2.14 am. I stumble into the hallway and turn on one of the many light switches and rub my toe and remind myself, again, that in the morning I'll buy a pair of slippers. By the time I get into Dad's room his breathing's a heavy rasp and I get him a shot of oral morphine, crack the top off an ampoule of ventolin and fire up his nebuliser. We go through the routine that Nick, the palliative care nurse, told us to do: think of an oblong and work your way around it, the short sides being an intake breath and the long sides being a slow outwards breath. Within a few minutes his breathing's calmed down. I make him a brew, white with one, switch on the radio on his bedside table and head back to my bed to lie awake and look at the Giant's Teeth of light streaming through the top of the curtains and onto the ceiling.

He has end-stage emphysema and has been discharged from hospital. The lung-function test has been cancelled, as has the scan to gauge the size of the tumour. All tests have been cancelled. He's home now.

* * *

Blind Freddie could tell you that palliative care in the home is different to normal care, but I'm still surprised by how much this is the case. The things I'm doing with Dad—the bathing and the toileting, the changing of dressings—are things I did with Mam some years ago but that was as a result of her long-term physical disability. There was no diagnosis of impending death with her and so we could have 'good' days and 'bad' days. With Dad there are no 'good' days. He is not going to get better, and when I lower him into his bed and he shakes his head and mutters, 'Jesus, I'm knackered' I have no response. I just stand there, maybe rest a hand on the round of his back as he gathers his breath. One time I just said, 'Yeah.'

It also means that we're allowed to be businesslike about his stuff. We might be watching one of those ludicrous mid-afternoon quiz shows that Britain specialises in when he'll say, 'There's a folder in the cupboard above the wardrobe on your Mam's side of the bed. It's got my gun licence in there. You'll need to get that sorted.' Or 'Get those ferret nets in the shed and give them to Raymond Braithwaite. He'll use them.'

And so oftentimes I find myself rustling through his belongings while he's parked in front of *Eggheads* or *Deal Or No Deal*. I feel guilty going through his stuff, knowing that he can hear the opening and shutting of drawers. If the dead have no privacy, then neither do those with a diagnosis.

* * *

In the morning I get him into the chair in the front room where we sit and wait for the racing to come on the telly. I make him his breakfast: two duck eggs, a whisky with a dash of lemonade, a spoonful of ora-morph and a cupful of pills.

It's Easter and there are lambs in the fields, primroses the colour of spilt egg yolk in the hedgerows. The first swallows are bickering on the telephone wires outside our house, the pair that returns every year swooping in and out of the lean-to garage to check that their old nest is intact.

There's an election in the air and to listen to Britain's politicians you'd think that the NHS was some budget-gobbling dysfunctional behemoth, but I'm loving the NHS. Today we took delivery of a hospital-style bed that rises and lowers and tips and has bars on the side so that the patient doesn't topple out, and a special mattress with electronically operated pumps that inflate and deflate little airbags so that Dad won't get pressure sores. One of the men delivering and assembling the bed is whistling *Bridge Over Troubled Water* when he arrives, which is a nice touch. I make him and his mate a brew, both white with one, and he starts whistling *El Condor Pasa (If I Could)* and I think, 'Fancy that. He likes his Simon and Garfunkel.' And then, as he pauses over a his brew and couple of milk chocolate digestives, he strikes into *Cecilia*, and I'm hit with the sinking feeling that he's going to work his way through the entire LP, track perfect. Indeed it is so. He's just starting *So Long, Frank Lloyd Wright* as the van pulls out of the driveway.

I had to clear the bedroom to make way for this special bed. I pulled the double mattress off the bed base and dragged it into the back bedroom, then pulled the base apart. There are four drawers in the base and three of them contained the kind of stuff you'd expect to see under a bed: spare pillow cases, duvet covers, shotgun cartridges, ferret trackers, car insurance correspondence from the 1970s. It's in the fourth one, the one that hasn't been opened fully since the built-in wardrobe was fitted, that I find Mam's stash. In plastic bags brittle with age I find the birthday cards and drawings that me and my sister made for her forty-five or fifty years ago.

I find their wedding album, which I'd never seen before. Does that sound strange? I've seen most of their wedding photos but only in small six-by-four size with the word 'Proof'

written across them. It had never occurred to me to ask if there was an album; I'd always assumed they were too broke or cheap to do anything other than get the proofs off the photographer and stick with them. I ask my sister: she's never seen this album either. When she comes to visit dad we sit and turn the pages reverentially, peeling back the tissue to reveal each photo. It's a small album and contains a paltry ten images but they're utterly gorgeous: deep, crisp black-and-white portraits mounted on heavy board. In the one of Mam and Dad cutting the cake, she has a lucky horseshoe with a black cat over one wrist and I find it here, amongst her stuff in a plastic bag.

I find the cards she got on her twenty-first birthday, beautiful 1950s cards. I find her pocket diary, West Cumberland Farmers' Trading Society, 1955. It's the diary of nineteen-year-old Norma: a list of films gone to see, of dances, of fellowship meetings for the local Methodist church. It's as bald a list as anything I wrote in my diaries but, being her diary, I find it as gripping as anything by Steinbeck or Greene.

> *Friday, 4 March: Went to dance at Coronation Hall. Smashing time.*
> *Monday, 2 May: Stopped in tonight. Heard Johnny Ray on the wireless: 'Whowee!!'*
> *Saturday, 30 July: Been to the pictures,* The Glen Miller Story. *Good!*

On Wednesday, 13 April is the first mention of Dad: 'Out with Doug. I like him.'

I love this version of her. Unlike my own things, which revealed to me a different story of my own self, Mam's stuff reinforces my memory of the person she was: a fun-loving gadabout who grabbed life by the fistful. Like her singles and LPs, her simple diary entries are distilled essence of Norma. One week in June 1955, a week in which she'd gone to the pictures three times and dances four times, ends simply with the words 'Have not been home once. My feet!!!' Yep, that's Mam.

And Dad's stuff? The same. The ferret net-making equipment, the gun with its huge 'moderator' that makes it look like something out of a *Terminator* movie, the videos and DVDs (*Lurcher Lunacy*, *Pig Busters* Vol. 6, *Get That Fox*), the small things that have something to do with hunting that I don't understand (hare whistles? fox callers?), they're all pure Dougie.

* * *

We don't get much use out of the fancy bed. Dad dies within a fortnight and before I know it the lads from the NHS are here to dismantle it and take on to someone else. They have the good grace not to whistle.

My sister comes over and we start packing up Dad's stuff, what's left of it. There's neither rush nor reason but it gives us a sense of purpose and makes our hands busy. We're both struck at how quickly his presence is erased; it's almost as though he was never here, in this house that he built with his own hands.

A real estate valuer comes around to assess the property for probate. He's very seasoned at this kind of thing and his eye moves across each surface and item as though it were on a flatbed scanner. Of Mam's beloved chipboard furniture he says, 'If it's a deceased estate and there's no one who wants it we usually flat pack it onto a skip and it goes to landfill.' The contents of the house—furniture, china figures playing barrel organs, miniature teapot collection, cutlery and crockery, bedding, everything—he values at six hundred pounds.

* * *

A lot of time has passed since I started writing about my stuff. As well as Dad dying, my son, the skinny teen I was bemoaning somewhere at midpoint in the book, has grown up, started uni, dropped out of uni, started work and moved out of home. The three of us who are left behind look at his room and each imagines it for themselves: a studio, an office, a spare room, a mini gym. The trouble is, it's full of his stuff.

I'm looking at it now. His books, from *Spot* to *Captain Underpants* to *Game of Thrones*; his huge collection of tiny plastic Warhammer figures, all in various stages of being painted or glued or broken; a guitar with a busted string propped against the wall; the glass shelf of the martini glasses, cocktail shakers and drinks that he wanted so badly for his eighteenth birthday; a stack of HSC workbooks; the wooden biplane produced over a term of Tech at school; the soft toys—Bunny and Wombat—who were his nightly companions for so many years before finding themselves relegated to the bottom of the wardrobe next to the crusted soccer boots and cricket hat.

I wonder about this stuff. It tells me nothing about the person who is now living independently, earning an income, doing things with friends that I don't know about and probably don't want to know about. It's just his stuff. I go to the supermarket and grab a few boxes and start filling them with the plastic figures, the Ripley's *Believe It Or Not!* and Guinness *World Records* annuals and the souvenirs of school trips to the snow. And I'm surprised at how easily it all packs down. It fills about five boxes.

A PROMISE

Names of people and places and descriptions of events have been changed. It's only fair; people with families, careers and a future don't need to be reminded of something dumb that happened decades ago and that I've either misremembered, misrepresented, embellished, embroidered or just plain made up, believing it to be 'a memory'.

In the boxes there were things that I don't talk about. If there's a postcard from Girl X or a letter from Girl Y then it remained unmentioned. It's entirely possible that, somewhere in a shoebox or cake tin in an attic in Leeds or Kirkcaldy there are letters and postcards that I sent to them. Would I want even one word of what I wrote in a soppy and testosterone-fuelled moment in 1980 to appear in someone else's book?

If there's one thing the contents of these five boxes have taught me it's the unreliability of my own version of my past. So if you think you see yourself in here, it isn't: it's just me forgetting how to remember.

ACKNOWLEDGEMENTS

Every writer has a particular person that they write for. My person is Christine Bruderlin. She raises my standards, picks the nits that need nit-picking, and makes me think twice before putting out anything that's underdone. Love and thank yous, as always.

Richard Lever provided outstanding feedback on a draft version of the typescript. As always, his comments were on the money. He has the ability to point out those things that aren't working in a way that makes you like him more for his criticism rather than less.

Trevor Dickinson gets it. There was only one person I would have asked to draw some of my stuff, and this book is elevated for his contribution.

Thanks to The Press Gang – Clark Gormley, Alexandra Morris and David Graham – for helpful comments on a draft of the introduction.

To both my children: thank you for being such good sports. It must be wearing, having a dad like me, but your grace and good humour allow me to get away with an awful lot.

MM 2015

About the author

Mark MacLean was born and raised in that part of Lancashire that's more Cumberland and Westmorland.

As well as his book and journal writing, Mark's blog on the natural history and antiquities of Hamilton North—the suburb of Newcastle, New South Wales, that he now calls home—is enduringly popular.

Other books by Mark MacLean

A Year Down the Drain: Walking in Styx Creek, January to December

The bestselling book tells Mark's story of his year walking a concrete drain in suburban Newcastle with his cairn terrier, Jambo. Equal parts diary, inquiry and observation, *A Year Down the Drain* invites you on a journey with the author into Newcastle's watery underworld.

'An enchanting read' (*Newcastle Herald*)

'Completely delightful' (Richard Fidler, ABC Radio National)

'The Gilbert White of the Styx' (poet Bob Adamson)

Listen to Mark interviewed by Richard Fidler on ABC Radio National's *Conversations* program.

The New Landscape

An anthology of short stories which includes 'Unte nthenharenye?', runner-up in the David Harold Tribe Fiction Award at The University of Sydney.

The Oldest Man in the Universe Goes to Groovin' the Moo

A delightful short story by Mark MacLean, with illustrations and type design by Trevor Dickinson.

Mark's books are available through the Hunter Press **www.hunterpress.com.au** and at good bookshops, such as MacLean's Booksellers, Hamilton, NSW.